Arguing with Care

Dialectic for a Democratic Society

Harry P. Reeder
University of Texas Arlington

Kendall Hunt
publishing company

Kendall Hunt
publishing company

www.kendallhunt.com
Send all inquiries to:
4050 Westmark Drive
Dubuque, IA 52004-1840

ISBN 978-0-7575-8010-9

Printed in the United States of America
10 9 8 7 6 5 4 3

Contents

Preface

Arguing with Care: Dialectic for a Democratic Society is a text designed to teach critical thinking or informal logic courses. It is designed to introduce students to the process of forming and interpreting arguments in their natural setting. Its thrust is practical: theoretical discussions of logic are introduced only to the extent that they will facilitate the application of logic to real-life arguments. This text is the result of years of teaching logical thinking with an interest in its being of use to students outside the classroom: in other classes, in the social and political arenas, and in interpersonal relationships. Traditional logical techniques, such as Venn diagrams, syllogisms, and propositional calculus, have been eliminated or pared down to a minimum. Any ideas or techniques that students have said they never used after the course was over have been eliminated in favor of concepts and techniques that have proven useful to students in the long run. In essence, I have allowed myself to be guided by the many students who have come back to me, often long after they took my course in critical thinking, to tell me just what parts of my course helped them in practical ways—with their mothers, their boyfriends, their bosses, and their colleagues.

Preface to the North American English Edition

This text is dedicated to my students. It was developed in over more than thirty years of teaching critical thinking at universities in three nations, at both the undergraduate and the graduate levels. It has gone through dozens of drafts, and the last page of each draft was a request to my students to tell me what about the text worked for them, and what didn't. As a result of their comments, I have made many additions and deletions to the text. In each draft my goal has been brevity and clarity, because I believe that the subject matter of the text is both extremely challenging and of great importance, not only in university classes but also in everyday life. But even more, in each draft my goal was to make this text *useful* to the students in their everyday and professional lives. I have deleted a lot of traditional formal logic from the text because students (including many former students, years after taking the course) have informed me that these techniques were never used after the course was over. I believe that a course in critical thinking should be not about taking a course but about helping students to prepare for their very difficult lives *after* the course is over. As I adapted my course more and more to this end, my students and former students have informed me that this text continues to serve them outside of the course and long after it is over.

My focus upon the everyday experience of argumentation stems in part from my belief that philosophy is about our lives and our world and was never meant to be an abstruse enterprise of interest only to experts. It also stems from my understanding of a particular philosophical movement called *phenomenology,* which was developed precisely to reintroduce human experience, as it is actually lived, into a philosophical tradition that had, by the beginning of the twentieth century, become so dominated by the natural sciences that human experience was deemed by many to be unfit for philosophical reflection. Indeed, reflection itself had become labeled a "merely subjective" enterprise that had nothing to offer either science or intellectual life. Edmund Husserl (1859–1938), the founder of phenomenology, had been trained as a mathematician (his first doctorate was in mathematics, his second in philosophy), but he became convinced that, because all human knowledge is based upon the conscious experience of living human beings, philosophy (and science) must sometimes focus upon that very experience, which includes, but is not limited to, the objective sciences. While constantly seeking objectively founded insights into living experience, he also sought to include attention to the contextual features of human knowledge, such as history, language, and culture.

I decided not to include any of the technical language, terminology, or themes of phenomenology in this text but to remain true to the phenomenological intent to base a philosophical account of something—in this case, critical thinking—in lived human experience. The focus here is thus upon argumentation as a *living process,* something that human beings do for a purpose (in fact, for many purposes). One result of this focus is an emphasis not only upon the logic of arguments but also upon the rhetoric of the human attempt to change people's minds, to influence others, to persuade them. Consequently, this text is not only upon the relatively stable *mechanics* of argumentation but also upon our living intentions and feelings that are so much a part of this living process and that change from time to time and from context to context. Phenomenology tells us that we should not ignore the full living context of our decisions, judgments, and arguments; and it is this focus upon the living, persuasive *context* of arguments that separates this text from most other texts in critical thinking. Although there are perfectly abstract logical rules, arguments are always addressed *from* someone *to* someone and always in a living context, which includes human purposes. While there are aspects of logic that are totally abstract and isolable from human experience (this insight is the source of formal logic and of computer chips and programming), the use and the *importance* of logic are not separable from our living intentions.

One central importance of argumentation is its role in democratic politics; thus, the text addresses this issue, including in its subtitle. I have been told by professional logicians that this focus is rather naïve, that logic can be used for good or evil. While I do not disagree with the latter point, I do deny that the teaching of critical thinking in a manner that addresses the argumentative *uses* and *practices* of critical thinking in a democratic society is naïve. Indeed, I agree with Socrates that critical thinking is not "value neutral" in a democratic society but is in fact both a personal and a civic virtue. This focus upon communal decision making is one reason for the text's blending of logic and rhetoric in addressing the human process of argumentation. Arguing with care is important because we must care for each other and for our society's group decisions. We can ill afford the "value-neutral" approach to argumentation as a social process, as this tends to lead to selfishness, technocracy, and cynicism.

I would like to thank Editorial San Pablo, Bogotá, Colombia, for the first opportunity to publish this text (*Argumentando con Cuidado: Dialéctica para una Sociedad Democrática,* 2007), and for its subsequent publishing of it in electronic form in English (to make it available for my students for one year at the University of Texas at Arlington). I also thank Kendall Hunt Publishing Company for its willingness to publish the text (altered somewhat for this first North American edition) in a form that is maximally useful to students. In addition, I would like to thank Professor Dr. Germán Vargas Guillén for his encouragement and help in preparing the Spanish edition and in making the English edition available for a North American publisher. Most of all, I wish to thank my many students who—having realized the power of understanding logic as a tool for their lives, their achievements, and their personal relations—encouraged me to continue to develop this text. The text is far from finished; in that vein, the last page continues to be a request to send comments to the author—who sees himself as a coauthor with thousands of students.

Harry P. Reeder
Arlington, Texas, June 2009

CHAPTER 1

Introduction

Critical thinking is not—and should not be, as we will see—a method for forcing your views upon others. Critical thinking involves being self-critical, subjecting all views—including your own—to careful examination and assessment. Learning to identify and to cope with your own limitations is a central feature of critical thinking. A central thesis of this book is that a critical thinker will recognize the value of fair and honest discourse in a democratic environment. The fact is that we need each other; no one knows everything, and in modern society the issues confronting us in need of critical decisions are many and complex. More than ever, we need to rely upon the knowledge of experts—experts that are increasingly narrow, isolated, and hard to understand.

Of course, we cannot take whatever experts say merely at face value: even experts can be mistaken, can lie, or can try to manipulate us for their own ends (or those of their party, their boss, or their lover). We have to maintain a careful balance with experts: we have to give credence to their opinions on certain issues, but at the same time we have to be critical of their biases, their conflicts of interest, and their nonexpert opinions.

Because the process of argumentation often involves deep-seated but conflicting beliefs, **logical skills** alone are insufficient to develop *effective* critical thinking and arguing; **rhetorical skills** are also important. *Logical skills* help to identify and examine claims and their interrelationships. *Rhetorical skills* help to identify and to examine one's relations with the persons one hopes to convince. Thus, in addition to logical relations among claims, we must stress rhetorical relations among persons. We must keep in mind that a logically persuasive argument may be rhetorically unpersuasive; attention to audience, wording, and background situation is necessary if the outcome that we care to reach is to be achieved. If we wish both to understand the relevant issues and to be persuasive in defending well-considered views, we must master the basics of both logic and rhetoric.

Perhaps the most common major mistake made by many arguers is to "ignore their audience." How often have you seen someone argue with others, only to insult and shout at those others in the process? How persuasive do you think their rhetoric is? Do you really think that they will "convince" others to agree with them if they insult them? Of course not! Much of the argumentative rhetoric that we witness is anything but persuasive. But *why do we argue*? Is it not to persuade others to agree with us? If not, then what is our aim in arguing? If people pondered long and hard about these questions, both the logical and the rhetorical styles of arguing would change drastically in our society. The following text will ask you to consider not only the **logic** of your reasoning but also the **rhetoric** of your presentation of these arguments in order to prepare you to **argue with care,** to **argue democratically.**

Both logic and rhetoric can be—and often are—used for both good and evil ends. In a sense, this text is "value neutral"; its skills can be learned and used for whatever ends. Nonetheless, the text will try to establish one value claim: that a certain approach to arguing about issues with others in a democratic context is better than other sorts of approaches to decision making, at least most of the time. The "good" approach is modeled after Socratic dialectic, practiced in ancient Greece by Socrates. One need not agree with all of the Socratic philosophy to appreciate the method of Socratic dialectic. This method is, put succinctly, to argue openly and honestly with others in order to find the truth (if possible) or at least the best possible course of action. Most of our arguing is about what we should or should not do—it is about action. Actions such as passing laws; fighting wars; or refusing to discriminate against others on the basis of their race, gender, or national origin are extremely important. Our lives are very political, even in a nation where, for many people, *politics* has become a kind of "bad word," standing for people who stoop to "playing politics" (I am not making this up; we all hear it in the streets, in malls, and in coffee shops). In fact, living without voting is, in a democratic nation, one of the options of "playing politics"—it is just as political as running for president. In a democracy, all of us—like it or not—are political agents. Many people are "turned off" by "political rhetoric." However, this rhetoric is (in small part) also logical, and the issues are as important as our lives, because they affect our lives. In a republic such as ours, members of the voting public have a wonderful and at the same time terrible responsibility: they are the people who elect officials who in turn determine the future of their government. Ignoring "politics" is a deadly mistake. Many people ignore politics because they are intimidated by both the logic and the rhetoric of the political process. This process is complex, sometimes bewildering, and often misunderstood even by experts. No wonder that common people often throw up their hands and don't know what to do (or for whom to vote). It is one central goal of this book to help to prepare students for dealing with real-life issues, political, social, economic, and personal. Fulfilling this goal, which is a step toward mastery over our lives and our destinies, is too important to give up, to leave for others to do for us. To be sure, we are all placed within constraints—constraints of historic, national, economic, geographic, and other such contexts. Nonetheless, the democratic ideal is that we are all political equals and, as such, deserve to be heard. Of course, this equality involves heavy responsibilities; we should not try to change the future of our nation and of our personal lives indiscriminately or casually. In a democracy, individuals should do their best to contribute to mutual understanding of issues and decisions. This is a civic responsibility.

1.1. A Warning about Logic (and Some Good Advice)

Students almost always find logic to be frustrating. Logic sounds so "easy" and "logical" when it is explained that students feel they understand it quickly—only to find that when they try to **use** it, it appears very hard and confusing. This situation is quite normal and there are good reasons for it.

1.1.1. The Warning

Logicians, because of their training, are often able to explain logical techniques clearly. They rely upon examples that are carefully chosen to clarify the topic of discussion. Therefore, students find texts and lectures in logic deceptively simple. The problem begins when students try to put these seemingly simple concepts and techniques into practice. Because most arguments we encounter were not written by logicians, these arguments are seldom clear and simple. In fact, the worse the logic of an argument is, the harder it is to figure out what the argument is about. People often leave important parts of their arguments (even their conclusions!) unstated, or they state them unclearly or ironically. Thus, when students encounter the "rough terrain" of logical application, they suddenly feel that logic slips from their grasp—things that seemed clear and simple in class start to feel obscure and difficult.

There is one—and only one—remedy for this situation: **practice**. Students should pause at each step in learning logic and try to *apply* what they think they have learned to actual arguments—lots of arguments, for all arguments are different due to their living context. A good place to start this practice is in the "letters to the editor" and "editorial" sections in newspapers and magazines. These offer a lot of short arguments on a number of topics.

1.1.2. The Good Advice

Take each concept or technique outlined in your logic course and try to apply it to a number of example arguments. When you run into problems (and you certainly will—even logicians do), take them to your logic class: ask questions, demand clarifications. This way you will develop a *useful* knowledge of logic (rather than a bunch of inapplicable definitions and formulas). To repeat: put your logical knowledge into *practice*. Develop your "logical muscles" slowly and carefully, just as you do your body's muscles. And note: logical muscles atrophy if not used just as do your body's muscles. Becoming a critical thinker is acquiring the *habit* of using logical techniques and of thinking critically about their use in dealing with problems and making decisions.

1.2. Learning to Be a Critical Thinker

How can one learn how to think critically? At first glance, one might think it preposterous to offer college students a course in critical thinking. After all, if they couldn't think critically, they couldn't have made it to college. In fact, there are things that can be done to help students, even good ones, learn general argumentative skills, skills that apply to almost any decision making, problem solving, and arguing. We all have rudimentary argumentative skills, which need guidance and training to be developed. This development is difficult, to be sure. But it can be done. The reason for this is that we all learn rudimentary argumentative skills merely by growing up and learning how to deal with others around us. A metaphor that can help to clarify this is that of **muscle building**.

1.3. Logical Intuitions and Muscle Building

We all understand that body building is a lengthy and difficult process, which nonetheless we could all do, if we so chose. We all have muscles that can be developed by "pumping iron" or doing exercises. Likewise, the process of growing up has left us with what might be called **logical intuitions,** understandings (often rather vague) of arguments and arguing.

Any of us can spot an obviously bad argument, even if we can't explain exactly why it's bad and don't know the logicians' name for the problem. For instance, consider the following argument:

> It always rains on Tuesdays in London.
>
> Therefore, it always rains on Tuesdays in London.

We all recognize that this is a bad (unconvincing) argument, whether or not we know that logicians call the problem with this argument the fallacy of **begging the question** or **arguing in a circle**. We already have **logical intuitions,** logical muscles that a "trainer" (a critical thinking teacher) can help us to develop and firm up. Just as the athletic trainer must learn something about what the human muscles are and how best to develop them, the critical thinking teacher must study the process of argumentation or, in the case of traditional training in formal logic, the structures of many different arguments.

Like muscle building, critical thinking is something that we never stop learning, if we persevere; with practice, we can keep honing our instincts and building our knowledge of better and better ways to prepare and present arguments. Also like muscle building, critical thinking is something that will atrophy or "get flabby" if we cease to put in the effort required to keep thinking critically. Thus, the purpose of this text is not to provide a *complete* instruction in critical thinking (something that probably can never be done by any book or course, despite many claims to the contrary) but to serve as a guide and an introduction to a number of techniques to help one to develop one's critical thinking abilities.

1.4. Argument as Paradigm for Problem Solving and Decision Making

While this text cannot teach you the content and methods specific to every field of study, argument analysis on the **dialectical model** (to be introduced in section 2.2) is a paradigm for the sort of process that must be carried out when solving problems in each and every field. Critical thinking texts usually focus upon arguments. There is good reason for this: the study of a critical approach to arguments teaches critical thinking in ways that help in a critical approach to problem solving and decision making.

The methods for verifying or falsifying assertions will vary from field to field, so this part of the analysis of problems must necessarily be supplied by study of subject matter and context. The analysis of the truth or acceptability of assertions depends upon the context of the assertions in relevant facts, values, beliefs, and situations. This is why **research of the subject area** is a necessary supplement to the study of general critical thinking techniques. Nonetheless, in every field, and in daily life, arguing, decision making, and problem solving have some **common features**.

In problem solving, decision making, and arguing, we must focus not only upon the problem or argument or decision itself but upon the **context** in which the problem or so on is presented. A sensitivity to context often makes the difference between a good and a bad (or a good and a better) decision. This is in part because many areas of argumentation, decision making, and problem solving are complex, with many issues and factors being relevant to the problem at hand. Taking a "wider look around" is thus almost always a good thing to do in such situations. Becoming aware of this and getting into the habit of explicitly thinking about the context of the problem can help critical thinking in any area.

Likewise, taking the time to **clarify** the problem at hand is also very helpful. All too often, we solve the "wrong" problem or make the wrong decision because we tend to rush into the solution of the problem without sufficient attention to just what the problem is. Once more, getting into the habit of explicitly clarifying and carefully formulating the problem or issue at hand is an extremely important part of critical thinking in any area.

In many situations we are aware of (or can become aware of, with a little trouble on our part) how other people have decided or argued in similar circumstances. It is very helpful to take the time to examine **related issues and viewpoints**, in order to take advantage of the results of other persons' judgments about the issue. We often clarify and hone our own reasoning by running our ideas up against the ideas of others. In fact, as is shown in section 2.2, this is one of the central features of the dialectical approach to critical thinking to be taken in this text. For the time being, think of the **dialectical model of critical thinking** as the process of clarifying and correcting one's own critical judgments by confronting them with those of others.

In any area of critical thinking, related statements share certain common and very powerful **forms** of relation. Logic focuses especially upon certain forms of connection between statements, claims, or beliefs that turn out to be extremely powerful and important in critical thinking, whether it be about logic, decision making, or problem solving. The focus in section 8 is upon a small but powerful set of formal relations between statements, claims, or beliefs that are very helpful—in fact, essential—to critical thinking.

All arguments, decisions, or problems are *about* something. This is the **content** of the argument, decision, or problem. The content shifts from problem to problem, from argument to argument, and from discipline or subject to subject. The relation between **content** (which is usually learned "on the spot," in a particular discipline in school, or from an experienced practitioner in the art, craft, or line of work) and the **forms** of connection between statements is essential to critical thinking.

These common features of arguing, problem solving, and decision making may be summarized as follows:

Common features of arguing, problem-solving, and decision-making:

1. Analysis of situation or **context** of problem
2. **Clarification** of the problem itself (in its context)
3. **Examination** of **related issues and viewpoints**
4. **Form** or connection between statements (displays connection between viewpoints and reasons or evidence provided to back up these viewpoints)
5. **Content** or truth or acceptability of statements

Having made the case for the connection between the focus upon arguments in logic and related issues in all problem solving and decision making, for the rest of the text we address the study of arguments (in their context) and the process of argumentation.

CHAPTER 2

Argument and Argumentation

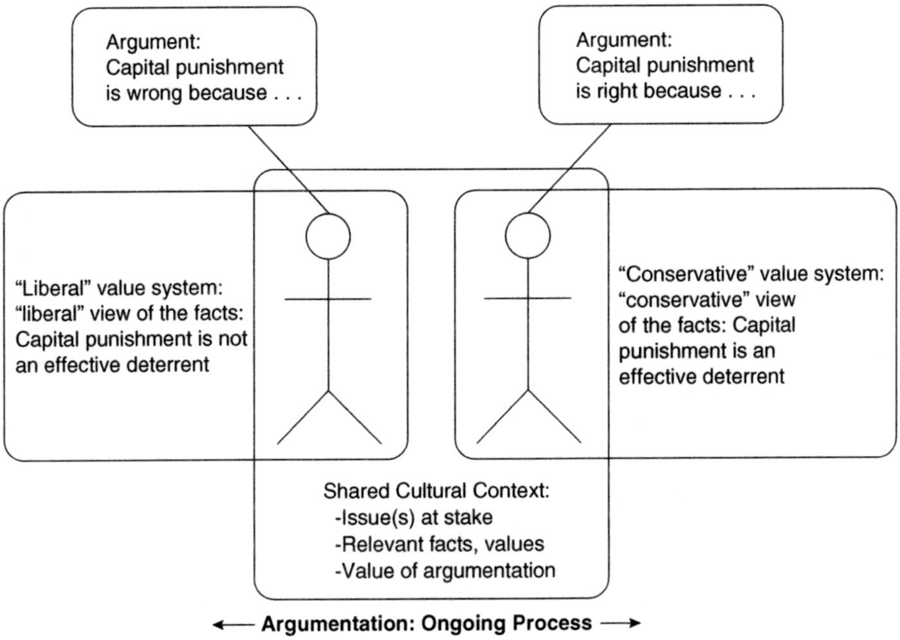

Figure 1: Argument and Argumentation

Although this text gives a lot of attention to analyzing arguments, it is important to recognize that much more is involved in analyzing an argument than memorizing and using a few "tricks of the logician's trade." Real-life arguments occur in a **context**; and in "real life," the analysis of an argument requires careful attention to this context. For instance, the claim "Americans value freedom" may in different contexts mean "All 'real' Americans value freedom," or "Most (actual) Americans value freedom." The latter claim might be a purely descriptive claim based on a sociological survey. The former claim might be a provincial value claim about construction workers (who often refer to themselves as "real" Americans, as if bankers, office clerks, salespersons, doctors, and students aren't "real" Americans). Only a **sensitivity to context** can help us to interpret such claims, to see what is really being said, because the same words (or groups of words) can mean very different things in different contexts. Therefore, it is useful in the analysis of real-life arguments to distinguish **argument** (a set of statements, often a written text) from **argumentation** (the ongoing process of arguing between people holding differing beliefs). Most of the arguments we will be analyzing originally occurred in the context of argumentation, and an argument's argumentative context must be kept in mind in interpreting and assessing the argument. Thus, it is useful to remember that what we call an *argument* is in fact a text abstracted from a living process of argumentation. Sensitivity to context is complex and difficult—but without it one often ends up addressing misrepresentations of both arguments and argumentation, and "missing the point." Sensitivity to context involves logic, rhetoric, background knowledge of issues and social situations, judgment about persons, and "educated guesses."

Argument: An attempt rationally to persuade someone of something.
Argumentation: The on-going human process of arguing.

2.1. Important Features of Argumentation

2.1.1. *Controversy*

People argue when there is **controversy**, that is, when there is something at stake (a decision must be made, a law must be passed, action needs to be taken, etc.) about which people disagree.

2.1.2. *When Push Comes to Shove*

We cannot support *all* of our claims: to do so would take an infinite amount of time. Therefore, we need some rule of thumb to help us to understand just when we need to support a claim with an argument. Basically, claims made in arguments (whether they are premises or conclusions) need to be defended "when **push comes to shove**," that is, when the claims are expected to be challenged. The degree of support required depends upon the degree of challenge expected or encountered. This is helpful in deciding which **premises** must be defended by **subarguments**, which are arguments within an overall argument that are used to support one or more premises. This is an important concept, as most people are unaware that the "nesting" of arguments within other arguments is important to understanding the nature of arguments; *each subargument is an argument in itself*, subject to the same laws of interpretation and analysis.

Subargument: An argument within another argument, intended to support one (or more) premises.

2.1.3. *Burden of Proof*

The **burden of proof** in argumentation usually lies with whoever wishes to change the *status quo* or with whoever argues for a view that is unusual or controversial. The burden of proof is the debt owed by an arguer to his or her audience. This debt is a *rational* debt, one owed to one's audience by anyone who tries to convince others by rational argument. This debt is also a *moral* debt arising from the commitment to relying upon reason as a means of persuasion (rather than, say, relying upon force).

Burden of proof: Because of the social responsibility of argumentation, one owes it to one's argumentative peers to supply reasons for one's views.

2.1.4. Argumentation Is a Beach

Above all, one should remember that the **role of the individual argument** in argumentation is a limited one: seldom, if ever, does one argument "sway the day." Because argumentation is a living, ongoing process, one must be aware that new information, new insights, and new issues may arise in a controversy, no matter what has been argued so far. Thus, each argument is like a grain of sand on a beach, and one might say that **argumentation is a beach**: individual arguments are joined together into platforms or belief systems (see more about belief systems in section 12.1), as grains of sand are built into castles on a beach. Like sand castles on a beach, which eventually are erased by waves and tides, individual arguments or groups of arguments may be toppled by further, future arguments or circumstances.

Argumentation is a beach: Because every argument appears within the living context of argumentation, a single argument, by itself, seldom changes anyone's mind—no matter how good that argument is (both logically and persuasively).

2.1.5. Shared Valuing of the Argumentative Process

Note further that, ironically, in order for argumentation to occur, the participants must actually agree on quite a number of things. They must agree (up to a point!) about what the issue at stake is, about at least some of the relevant facts and values involved in the issue, and—very importantly—about the value of the **argumentative process** itself. To argue is to agree to try to settle an issue with words and with (at least some degree of) rationality, rather than with force or some strictly emotional appeal. (Of course, many arguments we encounter clearly fail this last test—many an argument is left hanging upon *purely* emotional grounds, which are almost always *not* rationally persuasive). If one wishes to persuade someone else with an argument, it is not enough to express one's own emotion; the issue is whether or not there are reasons why others should feel similarly about the issue. Otherwise, one must merely shrug one's shoulders and say, "I just feel that way," without worrying about whether others do or should feel the same way. Much more is said about this issue in the following chapters.

Note that the value of the argumentative process is extremely important. If we agree to settle our differences by *rational* persuasion, it is a choice among various forms of persuasion. What sorts of persuasion do human beings use to influence one another? A look at history and at advertising shows quickly that we make only a few types of persuasive appeal; force (kings, tyrants, armies, terrorists), greed (political intrigues, vote buying, advertisements), sex (Why are all men and women in advertisements young and attractive?), popularity (Why do politicians call strangers "friends," and refer to them as "my fellow Americans or Texas, etc."? Why do we use famous actors, sportspersons, etc. in advertisements?), and reason. Given this short list of options, the appeal to reason appears to be very preferable in making many decisions, especially political ones. Thus the shared value of argumentation is indeed a backbone of the democratic process, whether it be in the political arena, in business, among friends, or in the home. Looked at in this way, the shared value of argumentation appears to be one of the most attractive options available to us as human beings.

> **Argumentation** itself, as a process of social and political decision making, has *value* in itself.

2.1.6. Logic and Rhetoric Intertwined

Remember that argumentation is a *human process*. As such, it involves not only our reason but also our instinct and our emotions. We need to be aware of our logic in order to offer rationally persuasive arguments. However, we must also be aware of the humanity of those with whom we argue and remember that persuasion involves more than just logic; a well-constructed, logical argument will not change people's minds if we use bad rhetoric in presenting our argument. This point cannot be overstressed: most of us, most of the time, argue in ways that are so rhetorically flawed that we do not succeed in changing anyone's mind about anything. Think of the sort of argumentative rhetoric you see around you day by day: people shout at each other, belittle one another, act superior to one another, intimidate one another, and so on. The real tragedy in this is that such rhetorical moves "close the minds" of the very persons that we seek to influence with our arguments, making it even harder to persuade them and, thus, *defeating the purpose* of argumentation itself.

Aristotle defined the human species as the "rational animal." Traditionally, logic has focused upon arguments and stressed the importance of rationality in argument. However, human beings have also been defined as "naked apes" by anthropologists who point out that our rational tradition has undervalued the very real animal nature of humanity.[1] In argumentation, we need to be aware of both facets: our rationality and our animal nature.

> In argumentation, we must keep in mind that each of us is both:
>
> a ***rational animal***
>
> requiring attention to logic
>
> and
>
> a ***naked ape***
>
> requiring attention to rhetoric.

With this in mind, let us take a brief look at a few concepts from traditional rhetoric: *exigence*, *ethos*, and *pathos*. We return to them in section 4.2.

2.1.6.1. Exigence. Exigence refers to the reasons "behind" an argument, that is, why someone is arguing in the first place. For instance, many letters to the editor in magazines and newspapers begin with a statement indicating the author's displeasure about some issue, article, or former letter to the editor, after which the author presents his or her argument. Because *context* is so important to

---

[1]This phrase stems from a famous book by the anthropologist Desmond Norris, *The Naked Ape: A Zoologist's Study of the Human Animal*, (Random House, 1999).

argument interpretation, we need to be aware of the exigence behind our arguments. We argue about taxes and health care because these are important issues that affect us all; we argue so frequently about these things precisely because we all agree that they are very important issues.

2.1.6.2. Ethos. Ethos refers to the opinion of the speaker's character that is set up in the minds of his or her listeners. In argumentation, this is extremely important, for if we cannot gain the respectful interest of our listeners we will be unable to persuade them of anything. This is why insulting or belittling our opponent or the overuse of irony can—and often does—prevent our arguments from having any persuasive effect, even if our arguments are logically correct.

2.1.6.3. Pathos. Pathos refers to the appeal to emotions that is so often present in argumentation. In one sense, we should avoid pathos, that is, we should strive to persuade others by rational rather than emotional means. On the other hand, we all have both reason and emotion, and we argue about things for the most part because we do *care* about the outcome of the discussion; in this limited sense, emotion is always a part of argumentation. To put it bluntly, since we cannot become computers we shouldn't pretend that this is somehow the ideal of argumentation. Appeals to reason are presented in the living, human context of rational, naked apes. Thus, appeals to emotion in a more subtle form are a universal accompaniment of all argumentation.

Important features of argumentation:

Controversy
Burden of proof
Limited role of individual arguments
Shared value of argumentation
Logic and rhetoric intertwined
Exigence, ethos, and pathos

2.2. Styles of Argumentation—Dialectic and Adversary Debate

How then should logic be applied? The "should" here is an ethical should, tantamount to seeking the good (not the evil) uses of logic. And how can this question be answered in a rationally persuasive way, that is, not simply as an expression of the author's belief but as an attempted **persuasion based in well-considered beliefs about facts and values**? To attempt an answer to this question, let us examine two different ways (one might call them *styles*) of handling argumentative contexts: **dialectic** and **adversary debate**. In order to distinguish dialectic from adversary debate, we will examine the goal, method, interpersonal relations, and results of argumentation.

In dialectic, the **goal** of argumentation is to find the truth or the prudent course of action. In adversary debate, the goal of argumentation is to win the argument, at any cost.

In dialectic, the **method** is an open, humble, search for the truth or for the most rationally prudent course of action in a given situation. In adversary debate, the method is to use whatever works to "win" the argument, to sway the audience. It is in this context that one often hears of "tricks" that play upon the credulity of the listener or reader. In dialectic, one admits one's ignorance and limitations (as well as those of others), the better to learn more. In adversary debate, one hides one's ignorance and limitations in order to sway the target audience. This is why dialectic examines and critically attacks **arguments**, whereas adversary debate often results in attacks upon **persons** or personalities. The calm and slightly detached mood of the dialectical arguer is useful to keep the argumentation focused upon issues and evidence, avoiding the sort of innuendo and personal abuse that are marks of adversary debate. This does not, of course, mean that in dialectic one must not care about one's subject matter (robots do not argue). The reason to practice dialectic is the passion for knowledge, for achieving intersubjective understanding of ourselves and our lives, and for prudent and proper personal and social decisions and actions. But this passion is a far cry from the kind of ego involvement in which a threat to one's argument is a threat to one's pride. It is this latter sort of emotion that must be avoided, for it inevitably leads to adversary debate. As Socrates has shown, we should be grateful for being shown where we are wrong—for thus we have increased our knowledge and found a further area for inquiry.

The **interpersonal relation** that predominates in dialectic is that of cooperation: all sides in an argument *cooperate*; they work together to improve everyone's understanding. In adversary debate, individuals *compete* to see who will be the "winner": one wins at the expense of one's opponent(s).

The **result** of adversary debate is that it weakens the participants. By swaying opinion on the basis of tricks, it leaves all participants still far from understanding and clarity and thus at the mercy of the next glib speaker or writer to come along. Also, by ignoring the feelings of the other "naked apes" in the debate, this form of argumentation *angers* opponents, making them even harder to convince and thus further polarizing the debate. Dialectic, on the other hand, strengthens all participants by firming their grasp of both the reasons and evidence for drawing particular conclusions and of the methods of rational inquiry (commonly called "logic"). Because logical skills may be applied to any subject matter, logic is truly a "transferable skill." Also, because dialectical argumentation recognizes the human context of the need to make

	Dialectic	**Adversary Debate**
Goal	to find the truth, or the best possible course of action	to win the argument
Method	an open, humble search	"anything goes"
Interpersonal Relations	cooperation	competition
Result	strengthens participants	weakens participants

Figure 2: Dialectic versus Adversary Debate

communal decisions, arguing dialectically appeals to the *naked ape* in the participants in a balanced and fair-minded way: if we are deciding what is the truth or what we *should* do, there is neither need nor justification for treating others as less than equal.

Degrees of dialectic and adversary debate vary. Think of the courtroom situation, which many consider to be a paradigm of adversary debate—and thus of a degree of sophistry. The defense attorney and the prosecuting attorney both try to win the argument and even resort to "tricks," the morality and acceptability of which are continually called into question, both inside and outside the legal and legislative professions. Nonetheless, it would be misleading to say that our courtrooms are merely the result of sophistry or adversary debate. The rules and laws governing the courtroom, the judgment of the presiding judge, and the precedent system all act as dialectical limitations upon the practice of any form of sophistry. If a lawyer refuses to abide by the conventions and laws, if she or he thus violates the basic equality and self-criticism of dialectic, that lawyer will be rebuked by the judge and or the legal profession. The restraints of "anything goes" or of "tricks" must apply even in a band of thieves, if it is to remain a band (as Plato points out in his *Republic*). The examples of *pure* dialectic or sophistry or adversary debate are extremely rare. Nonetheless, this distinction can be used to characterize tendencies in all argumentative discourse.

Our focus upon critical thinking will be that of dialectic. A **good argument**—whether or not it leads to the conclusion we expected or desired at the outset—will be one that **promotes dialectic**. For instance, one way to promote dialectic is to avoid overly strong claims, that are not rationally defensible, and to prefer smaller claims that which are rationally defensible.

Dialectic requires certain constraints, some of them moral and political, upon the arguers. To argue dialectically you must:

1. treat all arguers (and all interested parties) *equally*,
2. use *humility* to overcome inappropriate ego involvements (this takes a lot of practice to acquire),
3. work hard to *communicate* your view rationally and clearly, and
4. be as *self-critical* as you are critical (this is especially hard, requiring a lot of practice—and a willingness to make mistakes and admit when you are wrong).

In short, you must learn to *Argue with Care*. You must argue with care in your use of logic and rhetoric to promote communication and the sharing of viewpoints. You must also argue with care for your fellow human being, for only by promoting an equal sharing of **viewpoints** and rationally persuasive **support** of these viewpoints can you most faithfully support your duties as a political, social, and moral agent. A few comments on items 1 through 4 in the preceding list are in order.

About item 1: Equality—social, political, and moral equality—is important to promoting dialectic. Since we all have a tendency to hold our own beliefs, especially our moral ones, to be unassailable, we need to keep our moral, social, and political commitment to equality consciously in mind. This will help us to listen more carefully and sympathetically to the views and arguments of others. Of course, this does not mean that any self-contradictory or "stupid" idea is the equal of any other. "Equality" here has its limits and includes, at least, political equality and the sense of giving ideas a "fair hearing." This does *not* commit us to valuing or accepting just *any* idea or argument that anyone comes up with—these distinctions require *calls of judgment*, and we must always recognize that everyone's judgment is both *necessary* (if we are to make reasoned civic decisions) and *fallible* (thus the need for humility and for really listening to the views of others).

About item 2: Most of us, as we are growing up, find arguments pretty hard to deal with. In fact, many of us end up going out of our way to avoid argumentative confrontations. There is good reason for this reaction to argumentation. Think of your childhood, of how you groped with—and watched your peers grope with—the rules, norms, fads, and fancies of interpersonal beliefs and relationships. Think of how many times your verbal disagreements turned into physical fighting or bitter feuds. Of course, as we grew up we learned better ways to settle interpersonal altercations. (Please notice the irony in the former sentence! History and world politics show the irony.) In arguing, one often feels one's ego is at stake. Indeed, sometimes this may literally be true (for instance, in a judicial defense of a capital crime). But usually one feels more threatened than one should. Dialectic requires careful attention to the separation of **issues** and **evidence** from **individuals** and **personalities**. *Humility*—the recognition that your viewpoint is only one among many viewpoints, each of which deserves to be examined in the light of reason and evidence—is thus essential to keep dialectic from degenerating into the sort of adversary debate in which no one listens to others because each arguer assumes his or her own superiority.

About item 3: One of the hardest lessons to learn about arguing is the great difficulty involved in trying to get one's ideas across to others. Successful human dialectic requires careful attention to one's audience, to one's choice of words (indeed, even to one's tone of voice and gestures and dress), and to making the structure of one's argument as clear as possible. The field of *rhetoric*, stemming from ancient Greece, offers many useful techniques for dialectic. When **in an argumentative context,** always assume that **communication is a difficult and tricky affair** and pay extra attention to the requirements of making your ideas lucid, well supported, and persuasive. If you care about the outcome of an argument, dialectic merits **care in your expression** and manner, as well as **care in your logic.**

About item 4: There is a natural tendency in people to be harder on other persons' arguments and positions than they are on their own. Dialectic shares with empirical science an important rule of thumb: strive to be harder on your own viewpoint than you are upon the viewpoints of others. Any good scientist knows that he or she must test his or her hypotheses very carefully before suggesting them to the scientific community. The dialectical arguer will likewise be careful to examine his or her own claims and their supporting arguments *before* trying to convince others of their veracity or success (thus, the old saw: think before you speak or write).

2.2.1. Dialectic and Democratic Politics

In addition to having ethical dimensions, argumentation has political implications. Since we live in a world that increasingly values more or less democratic forms of government, the role of argumentation in democratic decision making is worthy of attention.

When one argues on the adversary debate model, one is placing oneself politically above one's adversary; in effect, one is arguing as a tyrant or slave owner, telling others what they should do or believe. While there are limited circumstances for which this is quite appropriate (for example, in some formal debates), in politics it is usually highly questionable, unless one happens to be in fact a tyrant. In a democratic or republican form of government, such an attitude is out of place; in fact, such an attitude is inimical to the very nature of a democracy or a republic, in which, in effect, *we are all in it* (the outcome) *together*.

Not only is arguing adversarily a threat to political freedom, it is also a threat to peace. Arguing on the adversary debate model tends to have the effect of inflaming emotions and leading to the breakdown of peaceful (dialectical) discussion. This means that adversary debate tends to **polarize** the discussion, and polarization of debate often leads to violence. Thus, the political importance of a dialectical approach to political discussions in a democratic or republican framework is extremely important: to argue in another way is to threaten the very political basis of the discussion itself. Therefore, although one may adhere firmly to the tenets of one's party, in the public political debate one must beware of inflammatory and divisive rhetoric, as well as illogical arguments.

2.3. Truth and Acceptability—Boulders in a Stream

A very important feature of the role of evidence in argumentation is its degree of persuasiveness; this includes both logical and rhetorical features. The **logical** feature is that the premises of an argument should provide sufficient evidence to justify drawing the conclusion. Weak premises will not persuade others to accept strong conclusions.

An important **rhetorical** feature of evidence is that it is presented to *persuade* a target audience to accept a conclusion. This means that, if one really wants one's argument to persuade, one must present premises that are either true (the preferred feature) or at least **acceptable** to the person(s) that the argument is meant to persuade. Otherwise, the premises will not help to persuade the target audience. To clarify the notion of acceptability appealed to here, let us use an analogy: boulders in a stream.

We can picture the process of argumentation as people on opposite sides of a swift-moving stream (there can be just one person on each side, or many). The goal of our arguments is to lead the persons on the other side of the stream to cross over to our side. In order to do this, we must place boulders in a stream, boulders that satisfy two requirements, one **logical** and one **rhetorical**. The **logical** requirement is that the boulders (in our analogy, premises of an argument) lead from their side of the stream to ours, that is, from the beliefs they hold now (disagreeing with us about the issue of the argument) to the beliefs we wish them to hold (usually, our beliefs about the issue). The **rhetorical** requirement is that we must place boulders in a stream that they will be willing to step on to follow to our side of the stream (that is, we must offer them premises that they will **accept** if we expect them to be led by them to accept our conclusion, which we already know they do not accept, since they are arguing with us). We use figures to illustrate.

In figure 3, person A has placed boulders in a stream to lead person B to his side of the argument, but the boulders fail the *logical* test: they do not lead to A's side, that is, they do not logically lead to the conclusion of A's argument.

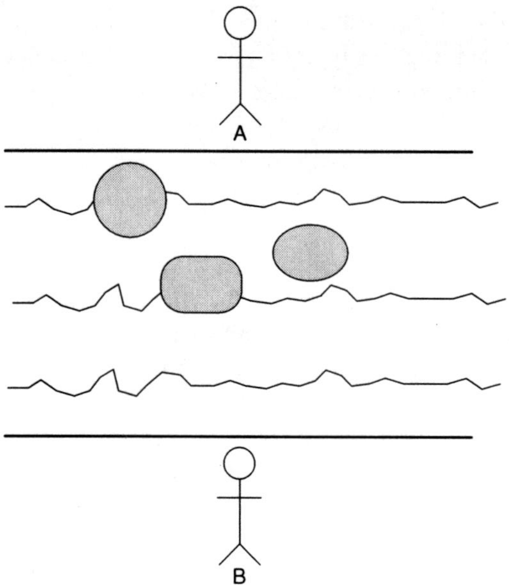

Figure 3: Failed Logic

Figure 4: Failed Rhetoric

In figure 4, person A has placed boulders in a stream to lead person B to his side of the argument, but the boulders fail the *rhetorical* test: they lead logically to A's side, but they are rhetorically unpersuasive because person B will not be willing to step on them—one is wobbly, one has a sharp point at the top, and one has a poisonous snake on it.

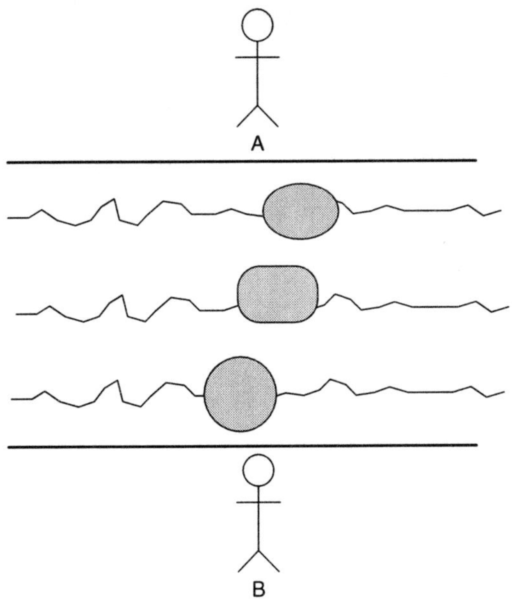

Figure 5: Good Logic and Rhetoric

In figure 5, person A has placed boulders in a stream to lead person B to his side of the argument, and the boulders pass both tests: the boulders lead to A's side (A's conclusion) and they are firm and inviting (acceptable to the target audience).

Rule: Use **acceptable** premises to persuade others of a conclusion.

This rule is indispensable to dialectical argumentation. Time and time again, people fail to be persuasive in their arguing because they don't think clearly about their "audience" and don't provide premises that really will persuade others. The net effect of relying upon premises that one's opponent will *not* accept is to "polarize" the debate. Merely repeating "old" reasons—reasons that have not persuaded anyone to change his or her mind—will not promote dialectic but will "turn off" one's opponent, rather like hearing the same abominable melody over and over leads one to "tune out" one's attention to sound.

This rule and the attention to audience and context behind it will lead **critical thinkers** to be **creative thinkers**, as they see the need to find *new* reasons, as well as new ways to express them, to help to persuade others.

Chapter 3

Context and Interpretation

The importance of context in the analysis and understanding of arguments and argumentation has already been stressed. The time has come to say a bit more about context, to explain why this is so.

3.1. Interpretation

Any time we "grasp" or understand an argument, we are performing an essentially interpretative process. Other individuals hearing or reading the same argument often understand something very different from an argument than do we. This is because the very nature of language necessitates the interpretative process when dealing with arguments (and, indeed, with any written or spoken discourse). The problems of interpretation led philosophers, philologists, and historians to develop various hermeneutic theories (from the ancient Greek word for interpretation: *hermeneia*). Our explanation of why this is so will be couched in three key terms: **polysemy, explanation**, and **understanding**.

3.1.1. Polysemy

Most words in natural languages have more than one sense or meaning. This is what *polysemy* means. It comes from the words *poly* (many) and *seme* (sign). Consider the word *ball* in the following sentences.

1. The umpire called, "Ball one!"
2. He had a ball at the picnic.
3. We went to the masked ball.
4. She's on the ball.

The first sentence is taken from the context of a baseball game. The second refers to having a good time. The third refers to a dance. The fourth refers to a quality of personality. Of course, in a different context, say that of a circus act, one might use the fourth sentence to refer to the location of an acrobat. Note that our sensitivity to **textual context** makes us able to interpret what the word *ball* means in these sentences; we know which of the many meanings of the signs (letters) in the word *ball* are to be interpreted because of the other words in the sentence in which these signs appear. In general, sensitivity to context makes possible the restriction of polysemy, which is a part of interpretation.

The word *context* covers a lot of different sorts of contexts. For instance, in interpreting the sentence "The umpire called 'Ball one!,'" we rely upon the rest of the words in the sentence to provide a textual context for the interpretation of *ball.* But we also rely upon our knowledge of the world, baseball games, and umpires to make this interpretation. The words in the text interact with our knowledge of the world when we interpret discourse.

This applies also to analyzing argumentative texts. In analyzing arguments, we will pay attention to grammar, to "key words" that appear in arguments (such as *therefore*, *thus*, *since*, *because*, *and*, *or*, and *not*), and also to the subject matter of the argument, the real (referential) situation(s) relevant to the argument (what the argument is about).

3.1.2. Explanation and Understanding

Given the polysemy of words, any time we interpret an argument or an assertion in an argumentative situation, we must justify or **explain** our interpretation in terms of the surface features of the argumentative **text** and in terms of its living situation or referential **context**. The process of explanation also can help to lead to a fuller understanding of a text. Let us examine this process in some detail. When we approach an argument, we already have *some* idea or other as to what the argument is about and what its context and import are. This understanding prior to working with the text can be called a **preunderstanding**. As we work through an argumentative text, doing the work of interpretation, we raise or change our preunderstanding to a new **understanding**, a new grasp of the argument and the issues it addresses. Thus, the process is a dialectic of explanation and understanding, which might be pictured as shown in figure 6.

We come to the argument with what is called a **preunderstanding** of the relevant facts, issues, beliefs, and values. As we read or hear the argument, the surface features of the text and our knowledge (our preunderstanding) of the referential context help us to interpret the argument. When the "going gets rough," we often are forced into a closer scrutiny of both the surface features of the text and of the referential context of the argument. In this way, we **explain** a text or a part of a text in terms of the text as a whole, other texts and of the referential situation

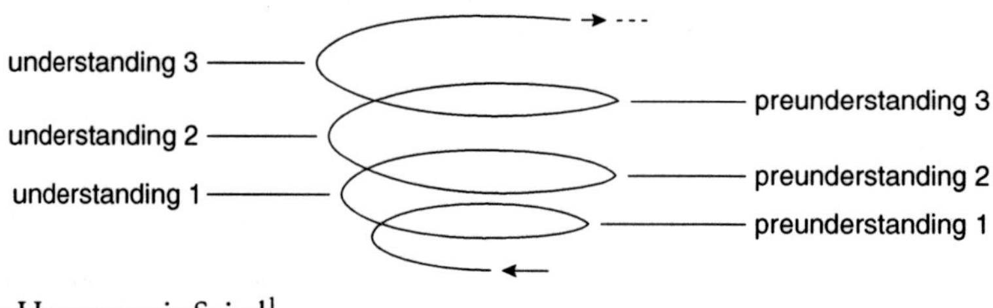

Figure 6: The Hermeneutic Spiral[1]

[1]This diagram, with a philosophical explanation and justification of its need, was first published in Harry P. Reeder, "Hermeneutics and Apodicticity in Phenomenological Method," *Southwest Philosophy Review* 6, no. 2 (July 1990): 43–69.

addressed by the text. This explanation in turn leads us to a deeper or fuller **understanding** of the argument (and often of the argumentative context as well). This new understanding may lead us in turn to effect a further **explanation** of some feature or other of the argument or its referential context. Thus, the cycle—**preunderstanding, explanation, understanding**, further **explanation**, deeper **understanding**, and so on—continues dialectically until we either solve the problem at hand (at least for the time being) or we get tired and set aside the task of interpretation for the time being.

3.2. Different Sorts of Context

We have stressed several times the importance of interpreting and analyzing an argument in its **context**. Let us now take this concept further and discuss several important sorts of context that sometimes need to be distinguished.

3.2.1. Textual Context

An argument is a text, spoken or written, produced during the activity of argumentation. In interpreting arguments, one must pay careful attention to textual context. Since the arguments in this text and many of those encountered in school and in life are written arguments, we will focus primarily upon written texts. We will rely upon clues from the text itself (as well as its context) in interpreting the arguments.

3.2.2. Social, Cultural, Historical, and Political Contexts

Texts are neither produced nor interpreted in a vacuum. In the preceding discussion of polysemy, it was pointed out that the social, historical, political, and cultural contexts provide clues in our work of interpreting texts. Most adults are very adept at suiting their talking to their audiences—at least much of the time. People change their vocabulary and even their tone of voice and manners of gesturing when talking with children, with superiors at work, and with their close friends. However, in the process of argumentation, people seem to lose sight of the importance of these contextual nuances. People often "talk down" to opponents in arguing, sometimes even adopting tones of voice and manners of gesturing that are appropriate for talking with children rather than with adults; it is no wonder that people often offend each other in arguing. Since it is the goal of this text to promote both good logic (proper reasoning) and good rhetoric (successful persuasion) in argumentation, we will need to be very aware of the social, cultural, historical, and political contexts of our arguments.

Argumentation is often unpersuasive not for logical but for rhetorical reasons. The social contexts of arguments can be very important to successful communication and persuasion. High-handedness and talking down are usually ineffectual rhetorical ploys in arguing. Sensitivity to cultural and economic differences is also important in arguments. For instance, the use of slang words may impress a popular audience with a speaker's awareness of up-to-date parlance, but the same use of slang may put off a more formal audience (like a class or a potential employer). While we normally do rather well in adapting to our audiences, it is precisely in argumentation that we most often fail at this important task. Because emotions, strongly held values and beliefs, and important issues are involved in many argumentative situations, we need to be more aware of the nuances of these contexts if we wish to be rhetorically effective.

3.3. Three Rules for Interpretation

Because of the complexities of the judgments involved in interpreting texts in their various interrelated contexts, there are not many rules that are almost universally applied. However, there are a few. A long hermeneutic tradition has established two rules, the **principle of consistency** and the **principle of plenitude**; in a more recent tradition, teachers and theorists of critical thinking widely agree on the **principle of charity**.[2]

3.3.1. *The Principle of Consistency*

It seems to be common sense that in interpreting a text one should not put any contradictions into the text that aren't already there. This, in a nutshell, is the principle of consistency, as applied to the interpretation of arguments. However, in interpreting arguments it is all the more important, because people's arguments often contain *implicit* contradictions (of which they are often unaware—this is what the *reductio ad absurdum* form of argument, discussed in section 5.2.3, is based on). This principle is extremely important when interpreting arguments.

> **Principle of Consistency:** When interpreting an argument, be sure not to *introduce* any inconsistencies into the argument that are not already there.

3.3.2. *The Principle of Plenitude*

This principle is based upon the PART–WHOLE relationship mentioned in the preceding discussion of the hermeneutic spiral. According to the principle of plenitude, your interpretation of each part of an argument (or text) must reflect your understanding of the whole of that argument (or text) in its context.

> **Principle of Plenitude:** When interpreting an argument, be sure to rely upon the *whole* of the text in interpreting every *part* of the text.

3.3.3. *The Principle of Charity*

You will only see or appreciate a convincing counterargument if you are "open" to it. This is why it is so important to try to be **charitable** in your interpretation of others' arguments. Using charity in interpretation is the only way to fully appreciate another's argument and position. The **principle of charity** is often discussed in informal logic as an important part of argument interpretation; in fact, it is crucial to it. Charity reflects your *attitude* toward the argumentative process (and thus is related to the *dialectical* form of argumentation). A recognition of everyone's equal right to argue for his or her view and everyone's equal responsibility to be tolerant of other

[2]This principle was first introduced by Nicholas Rescher in his *Introduction to Logic* (New York: St. Martin's Press, 1964), 62: "The governing rule in the reconstruction of enthymematic arguments is the principle of charity—one should, insofar as is possible, try to make the argument valid and its premises true."

opinions is important to one's ability to understand the process of argumentation. An intolerant person rarely fully comprehends opposing viewpoints. Composing arguments based on heuristic systems like the Toulmin Model (introduced in section 10.7) can be a lesson in tolerance, for if one seriously studies controversial issues at the levels of both explanation and understanding, one can learn not only about facts but also about beliefs and belief systems (covered in section 12.1). A careful focus upon arguments is one of the best ways to learn about the human process of argumentation. The principle of charity helps us all to overcome (as far as possible) our seemingly natural tendency to be overly critical of others and too easy on our own viewpoints and arguments.

Principle of Charity: When interpreting an argument, be as **charitable** as the content and context can permit.

The principle of charity is not as arbitrary as it might seem. If our goal in approaching argumentation is to **promote dialectic**, the principle of charity will soften our interpretations of the arguments of others, thus both enhancing our **ethos** in the process of argumentation and helping to avoid offending others with one-sided misinterpretations of their arguments. Recall that the reasons to promote dialectic include, in the long run, to improve mutual understanding of issues, views, choices, and the reasons for making such choices and the promotion of a rational and nonpolarizing manner of making group decisions.

CHAPTER 4

Logic—The Science of Argument

We are all aware of the many contexts in which people make claims; in science, politics, negotiating wages, and proposing new products, we are asked to believe certain things. Usually some form of evidence is cited to try to get us to believe the claims made. This is what an argument does: it offers evidence to attempt to **persuade us rationally** to hold a particular belief, to act or not act, and so on. Let us, then, define an *argument* (for the purposes of this text) as an attempt rationally to persuade someone of something.

> **Argument:** An attempt rationally to persuade someone of something

Logic is the normative science of argument. Its goal is to find rules or norms that separate good arguments from bad arguments. Logic is normative or prescriptive—that is, it sets limits for rational persuasion—because it attempts to discover not how we *do* argue but how we *should* argue (if we wish to argue rationally). A **good argument** is one that is rationally persuasive, that is, in which the evidence in the premises entails, requires, or warrants the acceptance of the conclusion (or renders it highly probable in the case of inductive arguments), *and* in which the argument is presented in a rhetorically effective manner, with regard to *ethos*, *pathos*, context, and so on.

> A **good argument** is rationally persuasive.

Logic is useful both offensively and defensively. It can help us to assess arguments that are presented by others, as well as help us to create more rationally persuasive arguments of our own. The techniques outlined in this text should be used both on our arguments (hopefully before we present them to others) and on the arguments of others. Being a critical thinker—being rationally persuasive—involves being self-critical.

> A **critical** thinker is **self-critical.**

Being self-critical is surprisingly difficult and takes both effort and practice. **Evidence** is what we rationally offer to others to persuade them to agree with us. We should always ask of our own beliefs, actions, and arguments, "Why *should* others agree with us?"

4.1. The Parts of an Argument

An argument contains two main components: a **conclusion** and one or more **premises**.

The **conclusion** is the *point* of the argument, the claim that the argument tries to persuade you to believe. To find the conclusion of an argument (which is often left unstated) ask, "What is the point of this argument?"

The **premises** of an argument are the statements that the argument presents (or tacitly relies upon) in order to persuade you to accept the conclusion. To find the premises of an argument ask, "What reasons or evidence are offered (or tacitly relied upon) to convince the audience of the acceptability of the conclusion?"

To find the conclusion of an argument (which is often left unstated) ask, What is the point of this argument?

To find the premises of an argument, ask, What reasons or evidence are offered (or tacitly relied upon) to convince the audience of the acceptability of the conclusion?

There are words that often introduce premises or conclusions in arguments, and they can be helpful in interpreting arguments. Although these words can supply valuable clues, one must not rely too heavily upon them. Many premises, and most conclusions, are not "signaled" in this fashion in day-to-day argumentation.

Words that often introduce conclusions: *therefore, it follows, thus, hence*

Words that often introduce premises: *since, because, on account of, due to, because of, owing to*

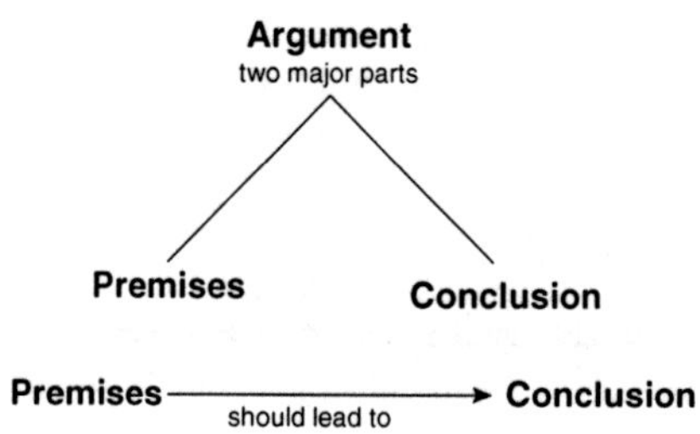

Figure 7: The Parts of an Argument

4.2. Logic and Rhetoric Revisited

You will notice that according to our definition of *logic,* the premises of an argument are addressed to **someone**, to an **audience**. Therefore, certain not-completely-rational (i.e., more widely human) elements of discourse should be taken into consideration in critical thinking about persuasive discourse, including argumentation. What this means for *arguing with care* is that our focus upon critical thinking will include not only attention to **logic**, to address the *rational animal* in us, but also careful attention to **rhetoric**, to address the *naked ape* in us.

Aristotle defined *rhetoric* as the art of persuasion. According to this view, our definition of *logic* resides within the domain of rhetoric as one particular form of persuasion, **rational persuasion**. Of course there are other forms of persuasion, the most widely used being those of appeals to force, greed, sex, and emotion. Most of us are persuaded to part with our wallets when confronted by a threatening gun. Most of us want to be liked by others, loved by some, and respected by many. As we all know, our emotions can conflict with our reason. The importance of logic lies in the fact that it singles out rational persuasion and develops our grasp of it. Few would want to be ruled completely by emotion, sexual desire, or the lust for power. It is the placing of reason in some sense "over" these other persuasive areas that characterizes our culture and history. In fact, Aristotle defined our species as the "rational animal," in the belief that it is our reason that separates us from other species. Aristotle proposed the following definitions:

Rhetoric: The art of persuasion

Logic: The science of rational persuasion

Note that in the preceding definitions rhetoric is called an "art," whereas logic is called a "science." This is an important difference. An art is learned—usually under the guidance of an experienced artisan—through practice. The practitioners of the various arts cannot explain exactly how it is that they produce their products, nor how the products affect others. A science, by contrast, is a logically coherent body of knowledge, knowledge that is learned by explanation as well as by practice in laboratory techniques. The scientist, unlike the artist, can explain how he or she works, what his or her product is, and how this product fits into our overall understanding of the world. All this is not to say that science is necessarily *better* than art; we, as humans, produce and develop both—indeed, we seem to need both of these important cultural forms (we need shoes and literature as much as we need penicillin and electric power).

In spite of the high value we place upon reason, our lives would be drab indeed without our emotions and other values. In fact, the famous Spock of *Star Trek* is indeed an impossible creature. If there are no other values than reason, and if there is no instinct, then there is no *reason* to survive. There is no reason to prefer healthy food to poison (or to not eating at all), unless one values one's own existence or one has an instinct for survival. (And are not instincts related to values?) Thus, to develop one's reason need not be at the expense of emotion or instinct; there is room in humanity for all of them, and we are probably richer for having all three. Nonetheless, there are clear cases for which we should prefer rational persuasion to other sorts of persuasion. (Of course, there are some very interesting not-so-clear cases as well, such as the role of reason in aesthetic judgment, which has been debated for centuries.)

By focusing upon the goal of arguments as rational persuasion of others, *Arguing With Care* invites you to craft not only the logic of your arguments but also the rhetoric of their delivery, whether spoken or written. "Bad rhetoric" is both pervasive in argumentation and very detrimental toward attempts to persuade others. Therefore, this text urges the reader to think not only in terms of such logical concepts as evidence, justification, consistency and relevance but also in terms of such rhetorical concepts as audience, ethos, pathos, and exigence, which were outlined in section 2.1.6.

This text assumes that the purpose of argumentation is that of *rational persuasion*. There are other forms of persuasion; rational persuasion need not be the sole court of decision. Nevertheless, there are clearly many situations in which rational persuasion is to be preferred. We should note that rational persuasion includes the notion of *persuasion*, which introduces an irreducibly rhetorical dimension to argumentation. A *practical* guide to critical thinking should therefore include discussion of the persuasive (rhetorical) elements of argumentation. Above all, it will be stressed that at all times argumentation is meant to be not only **rational** but also **persuasive**: arguments are produced "to win hearts and minds." Keeping this in mind will be extremely helpful in thinking critically about arguments and argumentation.

The purpose of argumentation is **rational persuasion.**

Some brief rules of thumb that are minimally required for rhetorically effective argumentation are not hard to find. We need to keep the attention of the people we wish to persuade—the **target audience** of an argument; to evoke in the target audience a sense of trust in our character and honesty (Aristotle called this **ethos**); to choose premises that we can demonstrate to be true, or at least that the target audience will accept; and above all, to avoid offending the target audience (a sure way to get them not to agree with you—in fact, not to listen carefully to you). Likewise, if appealing to the emotions (Aristotle called this **pathos**), be sure to do so only in appropriate ways (merely getting people angry or excited does not promote dialectic, although both anger and passion play a role in dialectic).

If you critically observe ordinary argumentation, you will see that people often treat each other really poorly in the course of arguing. They call each other names, treat each other as stupid and/or evil, shout at each other, talk down to each other, call each other names, and generally do just the kind of thing that **polarizes** discussion about an issue. This is especially distressing because the more debate polarizes, the less likely a truly dialectical interchange occurs. In polarized debate, people don't really listen to each other and they can't learn from each other—and the last thing that can happen is for someone to change another's mind for rational reasons. If you look at the typical polarized debate, you will witness the approach of violence. When argumentation breaks down, people lose faith in words and reason and resort to violence. Thus, our rhetorical strategies in argumentation are extremely important: dialectical argumentation requires not only good logic but also good rhetoric. Therefore, when entering into an argument, you should always ask yourself, "What is my purpose in arguing?" If your purpose is merely to vent your feelings, then you should not present these feelings as if they were an argument. To do so only "turns off" the people that already disagree with you, and you will make matters worse by polarizing the debate.

If you argue "to win hearts and minds," then the rhetoric of your argumentation is as important as is the logic of your argument.

> Adversary debate promotes **polarization**.
> Polarization often leads to **violence**.
> Therefore, promote **dialectic** by careful attention to both logic and rhetoric.

It is not hard to understand the point of these rules. Of course, we cannot rationally convince anyone who does not pay attention to what we are saying. Likewise, we should avoid inviting them to distrust us. Obviously, if we offend the target audience, it will not give us an attentive and open-minded ear.

> **Rhetorical rules for effective argumentation:**
>
> 1. Maintain **attention**.
> 2. Evoke **ethos** and, where appropriate, **pathos**.
> 3. Offer **true** or **acceptable** premises.
> 4. Avoid **offending**.

4.3. Claims

Before looking at arguments, let us dwell for a moment on claims. Arguments are logically ordered sets of claims—but all claims are not alike. Consider the following claims:

1. John is in the kitchen now.
2. All human beings are mortal.
3. Some women are as tall as most men.

Note that claim 1 is a **particular** claim: it says or predicates something of a particular individual. Claim 2 is a **universal** claim: it predicates something of all human beings. Claim 3 is a **general** claim: it predicates something of "some" women but not of "all" women (for it is surely false to claim that each and every woman is as tall as most men).

Particular, general, and universal claims function differently in arguments. To see this, consider the following claims:

4. John is in the kitchen now.
5. Some persons are in the kitchen now.
6. All humans are in the kitchen now.

Note that if one wished to refute claims 4 and 6, one need only point to one counterexample: if John is in the study, then both claims must be false. This is because particular or universal claims may often be refuted by one counterexample. General claims may not be refuted by one counterexample: if John is in the study, there still might be some persons in the kitchen. This means that just a little information is required to prove a particular claim: find John in the kitchen. More information is needed to prove a general claim: more than one individual must be found in the kitchen. *Much* more information is required to prove a universal claim: all individuals of a certain sort or class must be found to have the property attributed to them (in the preceding list, they are said to be in the kitchen now).

Many arguments are made unconvincing by **overstatement**: a particular claim that is justified by facts is usually not justified by these same facts if it is restated as a general or a universal claim. And the facts that justify a general claim often will not justify a similar but universal claim. For instance, when the **statistically** inferior results of females on some tests is used as an argument against allowing females to apply for a particular job, it is in effect treating the unquestioned inferiority of **some** females as an attribute of **all** females, which is surely unjustifiable. Thus, it is useful to remain aware of these different "strengths" of claims and to be sure that stronger conclusions are supported by stronger evidence.

Furthermore, many an argument is made unconvincing by introducing a universal claim in the conclusion, when in fact the premises support or justify only a general claim. This stems in part from a quite appropriate rhetorical style: ending the piece with a "zinger" conclusion. This often works well in lectures, stories, and letters, but it is to be avoided in constructing an argument—unless you are sure that you have sufficient evidence in the premises to justify a universal claim. So common is the "misplaced zinger" that it is a good rule of thumb when analyzing an argument to look for universal claims in the conclusion. Whenever the conclusion is a universal claim, be sure to ask if there is *sufficient* evidence in the premises to support it.

Universal claims are often, but not always, marked by such words as *all, every, each, no, none*, and *never*. The presence of one of these words in the conclusion is a clue to look for strong support in the premises. However, one must be aware that they don't need to occur for a claim to be universal. For instance, claim 2 in the first list in this section could as easily be expressed by the sentence "Humans are mortal." Even though it happens not to say *all*, it means the same thing.

Words signaling universal claims:

all
every
each
each and every
always
everyone
no
none
never
no one

A related but not always universal claim is signaled by the word *only*. This, too, is a powerful word, making strong claims that require strong evidence. For instance, if one claims,

7. Only the brave are free,

or the related,

8. None but the brave are free,

this implies that there are and can be no cowards that are free. Of course, without careful qualification, this is clearly false. To claim that there is only one way of doing something is to claim that neither now nor in the future will there be any other way of doing that same thing. This claim is usually unprovable and therefore could not follow from *any* set of premises. Therefore, look also for the words *only* or *none but* in conclusions of arguments, and be aware of the high stakes that they place on the premises of the arguments.

Words to watch for in conclusions:

all **universal** claim indicators,
such as: *all, only, none but, every, always, no, never*

CHAPTER 5

Form versus Content

In analyzing arguments, it is important to recognize two different features of the *success* of an argument: the assertions made by the argument should be *true* or *acceptable*, and the conclusion of the argument should *follow from* the premises. These two approaches are often called **content** and **form**, respectively. Argument **form** is important because many different arguments about many different subjects have essentially the same logical structure. Learning to recognize a few basic and commonly occurring argument forms is thus extremely useful. Whatever the **content** (subject matter) of the argument, its **form** must be logically correct in order for the argument to be rationally persuasive. We will come back to the problem of logical structure in considering formal logic in section 8.

5.1. The Two Challenges to an Argument

In effect, all assessment of arguments falls into two classes: assessment of **form** and assessment of **content**. Most of the rest of this text concerns answering two questions, called the **form question** and the **content question**. These questions (and not the mere words *form* and *content*) constitute the two challenges to any argument.

5.1.1. Form

The **form** of an argument concerns the relationship between the premises and the conclusion. It has to do with whether or not the premises establish or provide sufficient justification for the conclusion.

> **The form question:** Does the conclusion **follow from** the premises?

This query asks after the **form** of an argument. Note that the words *follow from* indicate a *logical* connection, which is different from *follow*, which indicates a connection in time or space. *Follow from* is a matter of the conceptual and logical **connections between statements** (between the premises and the conclusion of an argument). This question is answered by formal logicians in large part independently of the content question. Logic dwells at length on the form of arguments, and for good reason. Most of the time, the form of an argument is not signaled by the words in the argument. To see this, consider how unnatural the following argument is:

> I am trying to demonstrate that Senator Snatch deserves your vote in the upcoming election. My first premise (a ground) is: Senator Snatch has a better voting record in the Senate than does his opponent, Representative Grab. In support of this premise, I offer the following subargument: The first premise of the subargument (a ground) is: Senator Snatch did not miss a single vote in his tenure as senator, whereas Representative Grab missed seventeen out of twenty votes in his tenure as a representative. The second premise of my subargument (a warrant) is that voting in each vote constitutes a much better voting record than does voting only three times in twenty roll calls. The second premise of my main argument (a warrant) is that the candidate with the better voting record is the candidate that deserves your vote. Thus, Senator Snatch clearly deserves your vote more than does Representative Grab.

In fact, this argument uses surface clues ("my first premise," "the subargument," etc.) to indicate the logical structure of the argument. But of course it sounds very strange to argue in this way—in part because many people do not know what a "premise" or a "subargument" is. On the other hand, these clues made the logic of the argument very easy to follow. Most of the notational techniques presented in logic and critical thinking textbooks (including this one) are designed to make this logical structure stand out, so that students can develop an explicit knowledge of its structures.

In fact, we all learn to interpret arguments (up to a point) without many such clues, but our "knowledge" tends to rely more on instinct ("logical intuitions") than on firm understanding of logical structure. This text will ask you to analyze arguments very explicitly as to their forms, and it will present you with some powerful tools to make the job not only easier but also easier to remember.

5.1.2. *Content*

The **content** of an argument concerns whether the premises are true or acceptable (to the target audience).

> **The content question:** Are the premises, whether expressed or tacitly relied upon, **true** or **acceptable**?

This query asks after the **content** of the individual assertions in the argument, in their context. Logic alone cannot tell us if assertions are true. Knowledge of the truth depends upon conceptual, empirical, and other forms of research and verification.

In fact, we are all much more adept at judging the **content** than the **form** of arguments (as long as the content is not too complex, specialized, or esoteric). Thus, we will say more about **form** than about **content** in this text—because this is where we all tend to need more explicit instruction.

5.1.3. *Form and Content Interrelated*

In order to analyze the form of an argument, one must identify what role is played by the individual statements or assertions in the argument. This in turn requires that the reader or hearer must understand (up to a point, at least) the statements being made. Thus, a grasp of **content** or semantics is required for a grasp of argumentative **form** or syntactics. Likewise, the form of an argument can often help us to grasp its content, at least in part. Understanding the meaning of key "form words" such as *therefore, thus, now we can see why, since, because, not,* and *for* can help us to grasp the logical structure or logical flow of an argument, which in turn might help us to interpret a statement that by itself seems incomprehensible.

Since interpreting and assessing an argument rely upon interpreting and assessing both its **form** and its **content**, a few words of emphasis would be useful at this point. In fact, an argument's **form** depends primarily upon a relatively short list of "connectors," ways of combining sentences to form an argument. As will be seen in our subsequent discussion of formal logic, probably the key form concepts for our purposes are those of *not, and, or,* and *if . . . , then . . . .* We will see why in the following discussions. The **content** of an argument depends upon a grasp of the **key concepts** in the premises and the **conceptual connections** between them.

Interpreting and assessing arguments requires understanding of: the argument's **form** (*not, and, or, if . . . , then . . .*), and the argument's **content** (concepts and conceptual connections).

5.2. Contradiction and Consistency

A position or person is **inconsistent** when there is an implicit or explicit contradiction in its/his or her view. Aristotle's definition of the law of noncontradiction helps to show the nature of inconsistency: "The same attribute cannot at the same time belong and not belong to the same subject and in the same respect."[1] Not all contradictory assertions are inconsistent. A relevant change in circumstances can lead one to make an assertion that seems to contradict an earlier assertion. Also, as Aristotle's mention of "respect" in his definition of the law of noncontradiction indicates, one must also be careful about the different senses of words: some apparent contradictions result from a proper and acceptable use of a word or phrase in two different senses. For example, one might hear a high-school student say to another, "John is very smart, but he is also stupid," and realize that there is no contradiction here—John might be a straight-A student ("very smart") but a social outcast ("stupid") because he does not know how to get along with others. Thus, when looking for contradictions, one must keep the polysemy of language in mind and also rely upon careful attention to context.

5.2.1. Rational Discussion Impossible if Contradiction Allowed

If one accepts contradictory assertions from one's interlocutor, then one can never be sure of the meaning of his or her statements. Therefore, contradiction must be rejected wherever it is encountered.

---

[1]Aristotle, *Metaphysics,* Bk. 4, Ch. III, 1005b, in *The Basic Works of Aristotle,* ed. Richard McKeon, tr. W. D. Ross (New York: Random House, 1941).

5.2.2. *Implicit Inconsistency*

This is one reason for the careful laying out of what the argument is before analyzing the argument. Much of argumentation involves trying to make explicit the implicit contradictions of arguments and positions.

5.2.3. *Reductio Ad Absurdum Argument*

This form of argument (1) starts from premises stated or agreed to by a person and then (2) shows that these premises lead to a contradiction or an absurdity. If handled in a rhetorically effective way, this strategy can be very effective, but it is also likely to offend one's interlocutor if handled in a rhetorically clumsy way. Contrast "I'm not sure that I quite followed your point. Did you say that . . . ?" with "First you say . . . , then you say . . . —that just doesn't make sense!" In the former case, one leaves room for the other person to say, "That's not what I meant . . . " or "You misunderstood my point . . . ." In the latter case, there was no room left for the interlocutor to "save face." In fact, this is a very important general rhetorical strategy in argumentation, which might be explained by a personal anecdote: Once, while in graduate school, I lived in a house near a hospital. One day, as I went into the kitchen, I confronted a *huge* rat. I instinctively reached for a broom and chased the rat. I chased the rat into a corner, and then it did something that I had not really expected—it reared up on its hind legs and hissed at me, threatening me. As I was dressed only in a bathrobe, I quickly decided that I did not wish to do full mortal combat with this fellow at this time. I backed off.

In argumentation, it is always useful to remember the contrast between Aristotle's definition of humanity (the **rational animal**) and one definition popular in modern anthropology (the **naked ape**). Regardless of one's theology or theory of history, we are all aware that sometimes humans act like rational animals and sometimes they act like, well, animals. We cannot deny the fact of our emotions and instincts, although we all strive to keep these somewhat in control. Thus, the rhetoric of our behavior in argumentation should reflect our full knowledge of the persons with whom we are arguing. In other words, it is *rational* to recognize that humans are often *less than rational*, that we often act on *instinct*. Thus, to promote dialectic, the following rhetorical strategy is important in argumentation.

Rhetorical strategy for dialectical argumentation:

Never back your opponent into a corner.
For example: Always leave a way open for the other person to **save face** by either restating or modifying their argument.

5.2.4. *Contraries versus Contradictories*

People often find the distinction between contraries and contradictories confusing, but it is quite straightforward. The confusion stems from the fact that the first part of the definition of each of these terms is identical. Nonetheless, the distinction is logically very powerful, as there are only two alternatives in the case of contradictories, whereas there are often many alternatives in the case of contraries.

Contraries: Properties that cannot both be present at once, but neither of which *must* be true
Contradictories: Properties that cannot both be present at once, but one of which *must* be true

Example of contraries: Black and white (could be red, yellow, blue, etc.)

Example of contradictories: White and not-white (must be one or the other)

5.2.5. Paradox

Of course there are many *apparent* contradictions that are not in fact contradictions. These are properly called **puzzles** or **paradoxes**. Much of scientific practice is devoted to eliminating paradoxes. A paradox is an *apparent* contradiction. Paradoxes are invitations for learning, since contradictions cannot really exist. For instance, when physicists found a set of experiments in which photons of light sometimes appeared to act as particles and sometimes appeared to act as waves, they studied the phenomenon diligently. Why? Because they know that the world is, in a sense, logical. As a result of many experiments, physicists came to revise our understanding of what a "particle" and a "wave" are and started referring to subatomic particles with the term *wavicle*, to recognize that our ordinary thinking about particles and waves simply does not really capture some of what actually occurs at the subatomic level. Thus, the contradiction was eliminated by redefining or reconceptualizing the nature of the subatomic matter.

CHAPTER 6

Deductive and Inductive Arguments

According to a long-standing tradition in logic, there are two general *forms* of argument: **deduction** and **induction**. These two forms of argument are distinguished by their characterization of the *relation between* the premises and the conclusion of arguments. The main distinction between these two forms of argument is that in a deductive argument the evidence in the premises purports (attempts) to **necessitate** the conclusion; that is, a deductive argument, when logically successful, establishes a **necessary** relation between the truth of the premises and the truth of the conclusion. By contrast, in an inductive argument, the evidence in the premises purports to **support** but not necessitate the conclusion (we'll see why subsequently). Most inductive arguments **generalize** or **predict** from a series of examples, projecting that it is likely (but not certain) that other similar examples will be discovered to have the same features. If a deductive argument is sound, its conclusion is certainly true, but the conclusion of an inductive argument is at best probable. Let us look at examples of deduction and induction.

A deductive argument has a form that must be either **valid** or **invalid**; that is, the conclusion either does or does not **follow necessarily from the premises**. On the other hand, an inductive argument is never valid or invalid. However, the evidence in the premises of an inductive argument may be more or less **supportive** of its conclusion, so the form of inductive arguments is characterized as **stronger** or **weaker**.

In a **deductive argument**, there should be no important information in the conclusion that is not already in the premises; it is often said that the conclusion of a deductive argument is already "contained" in its premises. Thus, one test of a deductive argument's validity is to examine the terms and concepts of the conclusion and to make sure that they also appear in the premises: if important new information appears in the conclusion (but not in the premises), the argument is invalid. (Of course, information is often contained *implicitly* in the premises that is unrecognized until the conclusion is drawn.) In an inductive argument, on the other hand, there is always important information in the conclusion that goes beyond the information in the premises. Note: the terms *valid* and *sound* are explained in section 6.3.

Induction	Deduction
1. outcome (conclusion) at best probable	1. **If sound:** outcome (conclusion) certain
2. conclusion goes beyond the premises	2. **If valid:** conclusion "contained in" the premises
3. premises + **negation** of conclusion yields no contradiction	3. **If valid:** premises + **negation** of conclusion yields a contradiction
4. **Form:** stronger or weaker	4. **Form:** valid or invalid

Example of a **deductive** argument:

P1: All men are mortal.

P2: Socrates is a man.

C: (Therefore) Socrates is mortal.

Structure of deduction:

P1: Some assertion, when put together with

P2: another assertion (or series of assertions) leads conceptually to

C: some further assertion.

We now look at **evaluating deductive arguments**. As with all arguments, we must judge whether (1) the premises are true or acceptable, and (2) whether the conclusion follows from the premises. In the case of deduction, this second test is the test of **validity** or **invalidity**. Recall that when an argument is **valid**, its conclusion follows **necessarily** from the premises. Any deductive that is not valid is called **invalid**. To test for validity in a manner that relies upon your logical intuitions, read aloud the major premises of the argument and ask yourself if, *assuming* them all to be true, you are forced (conceptually) to accept the conclusion. If the answer to this question is "yes," the argument is valid; if not, the argument is invalid.

6.1. Two Forms of Induction

Most people think of inductive arguments as generalizing, or as arguing from particulars to generalities. This is misleading in several ways. First, deductive arguments often involve both general and particular claims. Second, people often mistakenly believe that any argument containing generalities—general claims—must be inductive. Third, there is another form of induction known as *arguing by analogy*. Let us examine inductive arguments more carefully.

6.1.1. Induction by Generalization or Prediction from Stated Cases

Example of induction by generalization:

P1: The sun rose today.

P2: The sun rose yesterday.

P3: The sun rose the day before yesterday.

P4: The sun rose the day before the day before yesterday.

Pn: (as many examples as you wish)

C: (Therefore) The sun will rise tomorrow.

Note:

1. There is no contradiction when the negation of the conclusion is combined with the premises.
2. The conclusion is at best probable.
3. The conclusion contains information (about the future) that is not contained in the premises.

Structure of induction by generalization:

DESCRIPTION of relevant case(s)

ENUMERATION of relevant cases

(Therefore) GENERALIZATION or PREDICTION

Note here that this form of inductive argument *enumerates* or *states* cases upon which the conclusion is based. A *stated* case is something that one can identify. Many people mistakenly treat general statements as indicators of inductive arguments, but one may reach a general statement as the conclusion of either an inductive or a deductive argument. Thus, the mere presence of a general statement is not an indicator of induction. Always look for the *stated* or *enumerated* cases, which must be present in the premises, if you think you have confronted an inductive argument. In section 6.3, we comment further on the nature of *stated cases.*

6.1.2. Induction by Analogy

Example of argument by analogy (the famous Cosmological Proof of God's existence):

P1: The world resembles a gigantic machine in its order and the miraculous arrangement of its parts into a meaningful whole.

P2: The order and arrangement found in machines were put there by their human designers [and we observe them in their creative work].

C: (Therefore) the Creator of the world must resemble human creators, in that He must have a creative, intelligent mind and a will to create.

Structure of argument by analogy:

P1: X and Y resemble one another in sharing common [observed] features A, B, and C.

P2: Y is observed to have feature D, which is unobserved in X.

P3: - by law of analogy or resemblance.

C: (Therefore) X must resemble Y in having feature D.

The argument by analogy works by comparing two things that we can observe and inferring a feature that we can observe in the one to be present in the other, although we cannot observe it. Logically speaking, arguments by analogy are relatively weak, based on mere comparison; comparisons are notoriously subjective. However, arguments by analogy are extremely important because of two features. First, an argument by analogy asks the target audience members to compare two things that they probably haven't compared before, that is, to see things "in a new light"; and this can be very powerful for changing one's view. Second, when we are confronted by something unknown, we always tend to analyze it in terms of strategies and features with which we are already familiar. ("What does this remind me of?") This is very important. For instance, HIV/AIDS was discovered because of an argument by analogy. Doctors began losing patients to diseases for which we already have cures; the doctors were puzzled by the patients' failure to respond to standard treatments. Moreover, patients with seemingly unrelated diseases were dying under similar circumstances. Researchers used the known fact that viruses infect different organs and systems of the body and thus cause diverse symptoms (think of all the symptoms of influenza) as a clue and began studying tissue samples from deceased patients. They looked for an unknown virus. In fact, they discovered a new biological agent: the retrovirus. With this discovery, they were able to identify the human immunodeficiency virus (HIV) and began research on treatments and a cure for AIDS.

6.1.3. Evaluating Inductive Arguments

As with all arguments, you must judge whether (1) the premises are true or acceptable and (2) whether the conclusion follows from the premises. In the case of induction, this second test is a matter of **probability** or **likelihood** that the conclusion will follow from the premises. Sometimes (e.g., in the case of horrendously expensive experiments in nuclear physics), we are willing to accept generalizations from only one case study. In such circumstances, the case is studied extremely carefully.

In evaluating inductive arguments, always ask the following questions:

1. Is there ENOUGH evidence?
2. Is the evidence BIASED or specially SELECTED?
3. Is the evidence RELEVANT?
4. Can you find ANOTHER CONCLUSION that might follow from the same premises? (If so, this weakens the argument considerably.)

Inductive reasoning is seen by many to be located at the heart of science. Science strives to explain the causal origin of events, things, and so on, so that a *scientific explanation* is the demonstration of causes. In experimentation, scientists test their hypotheses by running them up against nature. As we all know, nature admits of many *intervening causes* that interrupt expected cause–effect interactions (for instance, if you put your hand in a flame, you will be burned—*unless* you are wearing an asbestos glove). Therefore, scientists are careful to recognize that even well-established causal rules are never immune to being falsified by future events and discoveries. Furthermore, many effects result from a *combination of causes* (think here of the myriad causes required to put a satellite into orbit), so that even when scientists find a very highly correlated cause–effect relation, they can't be completely confident of that causal rule (recall here that inductive arguments can never *necessitate* a conclusion).

In assessing inductive arguments that are generalizations or predictions from stated cases, a set of three rules, known as **Mill's Canons**, is most useful:

> **Canon of Agreement:** Whenever the cause occurs, the effect follows; and whenever the effect occurs, it is preceded by the cause.

Canon of Difference: If the effect fails to follow the cause, or if the cause occurs without the effect following it, the hypothesized cause is either not the cause or not the sole cause.

Cannon of Correlation: The intensity of the effect varies in direct relation to the intensity of the cause.

To illustrate the utility of these rules, let us examine a few examples of causal reasoning:

Example 1: We all know that whenever gunpowder is ignited, it burns explosively—in this sense, the cause and effect *agree*. Nonetheless, damp gunpowder sometimes fails to ignite. Thus, we learn from experience that water *intervenes* in gunpowder's normal causal connection between ignition and explosive burning.

Example 2: Sometimes people who view a movie will attempt to act out a scene from the movie later on. In some cases, teenagers have performed terribly dangerous acts "copy-catting" a scene from a recently viewed film. In some of these cases, parents of harmed or dead children have attempted to sue the maker of the film in question, claiming that the film caused or compelled their children to perform the dangerous act. Such lawsuits fail, because if there were a *causal* relation between the film and viewers' actions, *every one* of the viewers would perform the same act. The *difference* between viewers' subsequent behavior undermines any claim to the effect that the movie *causes* such subsequent behavior.

Example 3: Scientists know that asteroids and comets normally circle planets or suns in steady elliptical orbits. Nonetheless, they often are pulled out of these orbits by the gravitational pull of *other* planets, suns, or asteroids, resulting in the fact that comets and asteroids from far beyond the orbit of Pluto eventually fall into the inner solar system, striking planets (including the earth), moons, and the sun. The *intervening* gravity of various planets in the solar system interferes with the normally elliptical orbits of the comets and asteroids.

6.2. Mixtures of Induction and Deduction

It is quite common to find inductive subarguments used to support premises in deductive arguments or deductive arguments used to support premises in inductive arguments. Consider our preceding example of a deductive argument. The premise "All men are mortal" was probably arrived at inductively. Thus, one might represent a fuller version of our original example of a deductive argument as follows:

P1A: John was a man and John died.

P1B: Bill was a man and Bill died.

P1C: Joan was a "man" (person, human) and Joan died.

P1n: (as many examples as you wish).

P1: All men are mortal.

P2: Socrates is a man.

C: (Therefore) Socrates is mortal.

6.3. Judging Whether an Argument Is Inductive or Deductive

In deciding whether a given argument is inductive or deductive, one cannot merely rely upon the table presented at the beginning of section 6 that distinguishes the two forms of argument. This is because, as you will note, the characterizations of deductive arguments in that table presuppose that the arguments are *valid* or *sound*. In fact, most deductive arguments that we encounter in real life are—as stated—invalid. Thus, it remains a question how in fact to identify inductive or deductive arguments. There is a relatively simple test, however.

> **To judge whether an argument is inductive or deductive, ask,** Is the argument a **generalization** or **prediction** based upon ***stated cases*** or an **argument by analogy**?
>
> If the answer to this question is **yes**, then interpret the argument as **inductive**.
> If the answer is **no**, then interpret the argument as **deductive**.

Important note: As stated previously, the appearance of a general statement or a generalization in an argument does *not* make it an inductive argument. An inductive argument is based upon *stated cases*.

Let us look at a standard example of induction: Because the sun rose today, yesterday, the day before yesterday, and so on, it is probable that the sun will rise tomorrow. Note that tomorrow's sunrise is very different from today's (yesterday's, etc.). As we all know, the sun might not rise tomorrow (it could go nova, or a huge comet could hit the earth and stop its rotation, etc.). Therefore, important new information is contained in the conclusion (as a probability, not a certainty). We use **inductive arguments** when we wish to go beyond present knowledge. We use **deductive arguments** to locate claims that are justified by what we already know.

Because the conclusion of a **valid** deductive argument follows necessarily from its premises, as we saw before, if the premises of a valid deductive argument are put together with the *negation* of the conclusion, it will lead to a contradiction. This is easy to understand. If the argument is valid, then the conclusion follows necessarily from the premises. If you add the negation of the conclusion, it will directly contradict the conclusion (which is already implicitly contained in the premises of a valid argument). This test for validity will not work on inductive arguments, since the conclusion of an inductive argument is never necessitated by the argument's premises (that is, inductive arguments are never valid or invalid). A deductive argument that is not valid is **invalid**.

> **Valid argument:** A deductive argument in which the conclusion follows **necessarily** from the premises
>
> **Invalid argument:** A deductive argument in which the conclusion does **not** follow **necessarily** from the premises

A valid deductive argument that has premises that are all true is a **sound argument**. The conclusion of a sound argument must be true. If one or more premises of a valid deductive argument are false, then the conclusion of the argument may be false in spite of the argument's validity.

> **Sound argument:** A deductive argument that is **valid**, and all of the premises of which are **true**.

Now that we have distinguished induction from deduction, and defined validity and soundness, a few words of caution are in order. In fact, deciding whether the arguments that we run into in daily life are inductive or deductive can often be a difficult issue. Persons trained in logic usually do better than those without such training, but even then the decision can be tricky, especially with arguments that contain *examples*.

Let us look at two arguments based on examples and see how to decide whether they are inductive or deductive.

> **Argument 1:** John Gurnsey, his brother Clarence, and his sister Melissa are all fine musicians, as are both their parents. It would seem that the Gurnseys have musical talent "in their blood."
>
> **Argument 2:** Liberal politicians tend to experiment with new ideas. Take Bill Clinton, for example. Thus, if our next president is a liberal, we can expect further changes.

When someone presents us with an example in their argument, they are generally doing one of two things: Sometimes they are using that example (*usually* along with other examples) to form the basis for a generalization, a prediction, or an analogy; thus are arguing **inductively**. At other times, they use an example (or several examples) as **illustrations** of some general point but are arguing **deductively**. In the preceding arguments, argument 1 argues inductively from five *stated cases*, whereas argument 2 argues deductively, illustrating a general point with an example.

How can we tell the difference between **generalization** and **illustration**? It is not always easy. Sometimes the author of the argument (whether spoken or written) provides us with clues, such as *thus we can generalize, for example, an example of this is,* or *sometimes consider,* and so on. More often than not, however, we are left without such surface clues. In order to appreciate the sort of judgment we must make to interpret these cases or examples, let us consider the *role* of examples in arguments.

Examples are used in arguments to make some general point, to exhibit a general structure. Examples can help us to get ideas across because they are concrete. For instance, if one is trying to explain what one means by a "conservative" in American politics, it might take quite a long time to explain all the features one intends (free-market commerce, loosening of central government control, "old-time" attitudes toward the family and social mores, etc.). Rather than entering into such a lengthy explanation, which might detract from the overall flow of one's argument, one might choose instead to use an example to make the point quickly. In using such examples (say, Ronald Reagan to exemplify political conservatism), one can make broad and complex points quickly. This strategy can be a good thing to do in an argument, but it also has its dangers.

Recall that an argument is addressed to an **audience**. In using examples to summarize general points, one must consider one's audience, to predict whether or not the audience will correctly interpret one's example. For instance, a Marxist might consider J. F. Kennedy to be a conservative politician, whereas some extremely conservative contemporaries of Kennedy considered him to be a socialist.

> When choosing examples to exemplify general points, CONSIDER YOUR **AUDIENCE**. Will they **interpret** your example in the same way that you do?

Having considered the difference between generalization and exemplification or illustration, how can this help us to interpret arguments containing one or more cases, if they lack the sort of surface clues mentioned previously? A call of judgment is needed here, since any case could be used in either way. Generally, however, an inductive argument based on only one, two, or three cases is very, very weak. Thus, the **principle of charity** (see section 3.3.3) would seem to be served by interpreting arguments containing so few cases as deductive arguments including illustrative example(s). In such cases, it is always a good idea to make clear (either in one's own argument or in one's interpretation of another's argument) what general point or idea is meant to be illustrated by the example(s) cited. In view of this, let us flesh out the two arguments we have presented.

Argument 1

P1: John Gurnsey is a fine musician.

P2: Clarence Gurnsey is a fine musician.

P3: Melissa Gurnsey is a fine musician.

P4: Mr. Gurnsey is a fine musician.

P5: Ms. Gurnsey is a fine musician.

UP6 (Warrant [this is defined later; for now, see the glossary]) [UP = Unstated Premise]: -thus, by induction,

---

C: Musical talent must be "in the blood" in the Gurnsey family.

We might sketch this argument schematically as follows:

Stated Case 1

Stated Case 2

Stated Case 3

Stated Case 4

Stated Case 5

(ASSUMED: these cases are representative or typical of many such cases.)

(Warrant) -thus, by generalization/prediction,

Conclusion

Argument 2

P1: Liberal politicians tend to experiment with new ideas.

P2 (RI): Bill Clinton is a good representative of many liberal traits.

IMPLIED (Warrant): New ideas bring political changes.

C: If our next president is a liberal, then we can expect further changes.

This argument might be schematically represented as follows:

General Statement

Illustrative Case

(Warrant)—Implied connection to conclusion

Conclusion

Having dealt with the distinction between induction from stated cases and deduction with illustrative example(s), how do we distinguish inductive from deductive arguments when they lack surface clues? The table about the difference between induction and deduction cannot help us much, because most of the items on the deductive side of the table are qualified with the terms *valid* or *sound.* Thus, one might automatically interpret an argument as inductive when it is really an invalid deductive argument. This won't work for us, because we are very often faced with invalid deductive arguments. What strategy are we to use?

The simplest way to make the decision is first to inquire whether the argument fits the definition of an inductive argument by asking, Is the argument a **generalization** or **prediction** based upon **stated cases**? or Is it an argument by **analogy**? If the answer to either of these questions is "yes," then we should interpret the argument as inductive (remembering to carefully distinguish illustrative examples from inductive cases). If the answer to both of these questions is "no," then we should interpret the argument as deductive (the question of validity or invalidity must come after the decision as to whether the argument is inductive or deductive).

> Is the argument **inductive** or **deductive**?
>
> Ask: Is it a **generalization/prediction** from ***stated cases***, or an argument by **analogy**?
> If so, then the argument is inductive.
> If not, then it is deductive.

Of course, we may always be wrong in our judgment of whether a cited case is merely an illustrative example or the basis for generalizing, as well as whether an argument was intended to be inductive or deductive. However, because induction and deduction have different forms of the **form question**, it is important to make the following distinction.

The **form question** for **induction**: Does the conclusion follow, more or less **probably**, from the premises?

The **form question** for **deduction**:Does the conclusion follow **necessarily** from the premises?

Now that you have a clear idea of the distinction between inductive and deductive arguments, let us turn our attention to formal logic, which focuses solely on the **form**, not the **content**, of arguments. The formal logic that we will discuss deals only with **deductive** arguments (although there have been attempts to formalize inductive arguments).

CHAPTER 7

Formal versus Informal Logic

This text deals primarily with informal logic. **Formal logic** studies universal principles of arguments, based primarily upon the form (syntax and structure) of arguments; it traditionally ignores rhetoric and argumentation. Our discussion of formal logic (and most formal logics generally) deals solely with the form, and not the content, of arguments. It further deals only with the form of deductive arguments. Its rules are stipulated or laid down and thus are *universal*—they always mean the same thing. There is little room for disagreement in most cases in which formal logic is properly applied. (There are exceptions, especially when the adequacy of translation into the formal system of logic is concerned.) **Informal logic** studies general principles and particular, general, and universal claims made in argumentation based upon both form and content, syntax and semantics. There is usually room for disagreement in the application of informal logic, as many **calls of judgment** are involved. Informal logic deals with both the form and content of arguments and deals with all arguments, whether inductive or deductive. Furthermore, informal logic has many rules of thumb and calls of judgment instead of universal rules.

Formal Logic	Informal Logic
1. Based primarily upon form or structure	1. Based on syntax and semantics (form and content)
2. Usually little room for argument	2. Calls of judgment, much room for argument
3. Universal rules (stipulated)	3. Informal rules, rules of thumb

Formal logic focuses upon the **form** of arguments by abstracting form away from arguments' particular contents and contexts. Thus, propositions expressing claims are broken down to simple propositions combined with formally defined connectives, and the propositions themselves are represented with P, Q, R, and so on, which are called **propositional variables**. These variables function as "placeholders" in formal logic—in just the same way that letters are used as placeholders in algebra and geometry: to stand for any number of different contents. The **contents** in algebra are numbers; in formal logic, the contents are propositions. Like algebra, formal logic focuses upon the rules of combination and separation of an argument's contents rather than upon the contents themselves. Informal logic, on the other hand, focuses upon both form and content, assessing not only the combination of claims (the validity structure or strength of the argument) but also upon the claims themselves (their truth, falsity, and acceptability). Because the distinction between **form** and **content** is so important in considering arguments, it will be useful to learn a bit of formal logic. (Recall that formal logic focuses exclusively on the FORM of arguments.)

Chapter 8

Formal Logic

The formal logical system that we examine is called the **propositional calculus**. It is a formal system for representing and analyzing **deductive** arguments.

Because most deductive arguments are based upon premises that make certain claims and that thus may be either true or false, philosophers have focused their attention on the forms of argument containing such claims. In logic, the word *proposition* is used to represent a declarative sentence that can be true or false. Some sentences seem to say the same thing and thus are identical as far as their role in an argument is concerned. Consider:

1. I am not proud.
2. It is not the case that I am proud.
3. Proud I'm not.

Note that all three of these different sentences say "the same thing": that "same thing" is called a **proposition** in logic. Thus, we may say that all three of the preceding sentences express the same proposition.

In logic, **validity** is a property of arguments, and **truth** and **falsity** are properties of propositions. A **valid argument** is one in which, according to its form, the conclusion follows necessarily from or is entailed by the premises. A **sound argument** is a valid argument with true premises. The conclusion of a sound argument must be true.

By examining the form or manner of connecting propositions, philosophers have discovered that some **forms of connection** of propositions are valid independently of the truth or falsity of the propositions involved. For this reason, symbolic logic treats propositions as mere algebraic variables called **propositional variables** and focuses upon the manner of connecting such variables. Generally speaking, P, Q, R, and so on are used to represent propositions, that is, are used as propositional variables. Various constant methods of combining propositions called **operators** have been defined so as to fit (as nearly as possible) sentential connectives in English (German, Spanish, etc.). The operators that we will use are "~," "&," "v," "→," and "↔." These operators enable us to express compound propositions.

"~" means "not" or "it is false that . . ." or "it is not the case that . . ." and is called the **negation** operator. When a proposition is negated twice (~~P or "it is false that it is false that P") we will consider it to be affirmed (P, or "P is true," or "P holds").

"&" means "and" and is called the **conjunction** operator. Thus, "P&Q" means "P and Q" or "Proposition P is true and proposition Q is true." Propositions P and Q in this case are called **conjuncts**.

"v" means "or" and is called the **disjunction** operator. Thus, "PvQ" means "P or Q" in the sense that either P or Q or both P and Q are true or hold. Propositions P and Q in this case are called **disjuncts**. If the sense of a statement is such that it excludes the case in which both P and Q are true, we may represent this statement by "PvQ and ~(P&Q)" or "(PvQ)&~(P&Q)."

"→" means "implies" or "if . . . , then . . ." or "follows from" and is called the **implication** operator. "P→Q" means "P implies Q" or "If P, then Q" or "Q follows from P." In an implication, or *conditional* (say, P→Q), the first term (P) is called the **antecedent** and the second term (Q) is called the **consequent**.

"↔" means "is equivalent to" or "is logically equivalent to" or "may be substituted for" and is called the **biconditional** operator, since "P↔Q" says the same as "(P→Q)& (Q→P)."

These symbols may be used in combination:

"P&~Q" means "P and not-Q."

"P→~Q" means "If P, then not-Q."

"~PvQ" means "not-P or Q."

To avoid confusion, parentheses are sometimes required:

"P&(Q→~P)" means "P and (Q implies not-P)."

"~(P→Q)vR" means "It is false that (P implies Q) or R."

"Pv(QvP)" means "P or (Q or P)."

Symbol	Meaning
~	not
&	and
v	or
→	If . . . , then . . .
↔	if and only if

Now let us see how ordinary sentences are translated into symbols. To begin with, it is necessary to set up a TRANSLATION TABLE to show what propositions are being represented by the propositional variables. It is not necessary to do so for the operators since their meanings are consistent.

Ex. 1: If the home team wins, I'll kill myself.

P: The home team wins.

Q: I kill myself.

P→Q

Note that in our first example the "then" of the "if . . . , then . . ." statement was unexpressed. This often happens in colloquial English. This does not change the conditional nature of the statement. Also note that the tense of Q has been changed to the present. This is because in our simple logic we cannot deal with the complicated notions of time and tense.

Ex. 2: If I were a woman, I would not wear a miniskirt.

P: I am a woman.

Q: I wear a miniskirt.

P→~Q (~P understood).

Note that the subjunctive tense (*were, would*) is used in English (and in some other languages) to represent a contrary-to-fact conditional. This means that there is a conditional being expressed, but that it is known to be false. Thus, out of this simple sentence, we can get two statements: "P→~Q" and "~P." Note also that we cannot get ~~Q, or Q. (Although it is true that I am not a woman, it is not true that I will wear a miniskirt.)

Ex. 3: If the home team wins or even ties, I'll jump and shout unless I'm sick.

P: The home team wins.

Q: The home team ties.

R: I jump.

S: I shout.

T: I am sick.

(PvQ)→[~T→(R&S)]

Conjunctions such as "R&S" need not be separated by parentheses or brackets except where important to the argument or statement. Since, however, it is often impossible to tell the importance of such conjunctions *before* we recognize the structure of an argument or statement, it is a good rule of thumb to break down a sentence as far as possible at the outset. Note further that "A unless B" means in effect that if B doesn't hold (is false), then A holds (is true) or "~B→A."

Because of the importance of knowing which argument forms are valid and which are invalid, logicians have developed a straightforward method of analyzing arguments called **truth tables**, based on a truth—functional analysis of propositions.

8.1. Truth Tables

A truth table shows the possibilities of truth and falsity of a proposition whether it be simple or compound based on the truth and falsity of the propositions involved. The truth tables for the compound propositions constructed with the operators that we will use are as follows.

P	~P
T	F
F	T

P	Q	P&Q	PvQ	P→Q	P↔Q
T	T	T	T	T	T
T	F	F	T	F	F
F	T	F	T	T	F
F	F	F	F	T	T

An entire argument may be stated in the form of one compound proposition, with the premises conjoined by *and(s)* and taken together as the antecedent of a conditional, with the conclusion of the argument taken as the consequent. Thus a truth-functional analysis may be constructed for arguments, based on the preceding truth tables. Because an argument form is valid (but not sound) independently of the truth or falsity of the propositions contained in it, an argument form whose truth table shows that the implication from antecedent to consequent is true in all cases is a **valid argument form.** (Remember that a truth table shows all the possible combinations of truth and falsity of a proposition, whether simple or compound.)

A truth table will contain **2^n lines** where "n" is the number of different propositional variables involved. (The 2 comes from the fact that there are two possibilities of truth and falsity for each propositional variable: T or F.) Thus, if there are three propositional variables—P, Q, and R, the truth table will contain $2^3 = 2 \times 2 \times 2 = 8$ lines. Therefore, truth tables provide a **test for validity** of argument forms.

Ex.: **Modus Ponens** (a valid argument form)

P→Q
P
———
Q

This argument may be rewritten: [(P→Q)&P]→Q. Let us test it with a truth table:

P	Q	P→Q	(P→Q)&P	[(P→Q)&P]→Q
T	T	T	T	T
T	F	F	F	T
F	T	T	F	T
F	F	T	F	T

Note that this table shows **modus ponens** to be a valid argument form, true in all possible combinations of truth and falsity of the propositions involved.

The following argument forms are all valid. Construct truth tables to demonstrate the validity of each one.

Valid Argument Forms

Modus Ponens, or affirmation of the antecedent (M.P.)

P→Q
P
―――
Q

Modus Tollens or denial of the consequent (M.T.)

P→Q
~Q
―――
~P

Disjunctive Syllogism (D.S.)

PvQ
~P or (~Q)
―――
Q or (P)

Hypothetical Syllogism

P→Q
Q→R
―――
P→R

8.2. Logical Equivalences

Name of Law	**Formula for Law**
Double Negation (D.N.)	P↔~~P
Association (Ass.)	[Pv(QvR)]↔[(PvQ)vR] and [P&(Q&R)]↔[(P&Q)&R]
Commutation (Comm.)	(PvQ)↔(QvP) and (P&Q)↔(Q&P)
Implication (Imp.)	(P→Q)↔~(P&~Q) and (P→Q)→(~PvQ)
Exportation (Exp.)	[P→(Q→R)]↔[(P&Q)→R]
De Morgan's Laws (DeM.)	~(P&Q)(~Pv~Q) and ~(PvQ)↔(~P&~Q)
Distribution (Dist.)	[P&(QvR)]↔[(P&Q)v(P&R)] and [Pv(Q&R)]↔[(PvQ)&(PvR)]
Biconditional (Bicon.)	(P↔Q)↔[(P→Q)&(Q→P)] and (P↔Q)↔[(P&Q)v(~P&~Q)]

Now that we have demonstrated the validity of various argument forms, we may use these rules in demonstrating the validity of various arguments. These demonstrations may take various forms. We'll look at **deduction**, **indirect proof**, **conditional proof**, and **logical analogy**.

8.3. Deduction

In a deduction, a conclusion is reached by a series of steps, each of which is justified by being (1) a premise or (2) an instance of a valid argument form or (3) a logical equivalence of a former step. By convention, the steps in a proof are numbered, each step being listed on a separate line. The step lists what is achieved, along with the justification for it, citing (1), (2), or (3), and any previous lines used.

Example: If Bill studies hard, then he will pass unless he is unlucky. Bill studies hard but fails. Therefore, he is unlucky.

Translation table: P: Bill studies hard.
Q: Bill passes.
R: Bill is unlucky.

Deduction:

1. P→(~R→Q)	Premise/Therefore R
2. P&~Q	Premise
3. P	2, Simp.
4. ~R→Q	1, 3, M.P.
5. ~Q	2, Simp.
6. ~~R	4, 5, M.T.
7. R	6, D.N.

8.4. Indirect Proof

In an indirect proof, an argument is shown to be valid by adding to the premises a further premise that is the negation of the conclusion and then deriving an explicit contradiction from the new set of premises.

Example: If John devotes time to philosophy, then either he will learn or he is stupid. After much effort at philosophy, John learns. Therefore, John is not stupid.

Translation table: P: John devotes time to philosophy.
Q: John learns.
R: John is stupid.

Deduction:

1. P→[(QvR)&~(Q&R)]	Premise/Therefore ~R
2. P&Q	Premise
3. R	Indirect premise
4. P	2, Simp.
5. (QvR)&~(Q&R)	1, 4, M.P.
6. ~(Q&R)	5, Simp.
7. Q	2, Simp.
8. Q&R	3, 7, Adj.
9. ~R	3–8, Indirect Proof

Note that lines 6 and 8 contradict one another and that the contradiction was arrived at through assuming ~~R, that is, R. Prove the same argument by a deduction.

8.5. Conditional Proof

An argument that has a conditional (if . . . , then . . .) conclusion is valid if and only if it is possible to deduce the consequent of the conclusion from the set of premises with the additional premise of the antecedent of the conclusion.

Example: If Tom drinks a lot, he'll get drunk. If Tom drinks a lot, then he'll slur his speech. So if he drinks a lot, he'll get drunk and slur his speech.

Translation table: P: Tom drinks a lot.
Q: Tom gets drunk.
R: Tom slurs his speech.

Deduction:

1. P→Q	Premise/Therefore P→(Q&R)
2. P→R	Premise
3. P	Conditional Premise
4. Q	1, 3, M.P.
5. R	2, 3, M.P.
6. Q&R	4, 5, Adj.
7. P→(Q&R)	3–6, Conditional Proof

8.6. Logical Analogy

This form of argument analysis is not, technically speaking, a part of formal logic, since it utilizes the natural language of argument (English, Spanish, etc.). It is included in this section of the present text because it is based in and focuses upon the **form** of arguments. Thus, although it is really part of informal logical analysis, its emphasis upon argument form makes it fall naturally into this section.

This form of logical analysis can demonstrate only the **invalidity**, not the validity, of an argument. The technique is rather simple to explain but is in practice rather tricky to apply. It is nonetheless a very useful technique to master as we shall see. Basically, this technique consists of identifying the logical structure of a perplexing argument and trying to construct a less baffling argument of the same form. Since we are trying to prove the invalidity, not the validity, of the argument, we will try to construct an *obviously invalid* argument of the same form. Since a valid argument form is one in which true premises force a true conclusion (valid form plus true premises equal **sound** argument), our attempt to construct an invalid argument of the same form consists of trying to think up an argument of the same form that has obviously true premises and an obviously false conclusion. If we can think of such a case, this proves the argument form to be invalid. We cannot prove validity in this manner since there are, in principle, an infinite number of arguments of the same form, and any one of these arguments might turn out to be invalid. Consider the following argument:

P1: All murder is wrong.
P2: Abortion is wrong.
____
Therefore, all abortion is murder.

Is this argument valid? Many of us are not sure at the outset. The technique of logical analogy makes it easy to see why this argument is invalid. This technique is based on the form or structure of the argument. Let us look at this argument's structure, that is, let us examine its claims without interest in the content or topic of the argument. Basically, the argument says structurally the following:

P1: All X is Y.
P2: All Z is Y.
____
Therefore, all Z is X.

Now let us *recast* the argument with obviously true premises and an obviously false conclusion:

P1: All dogs are animals.
P2: All cats are animals.
____
Therefore, all cats are dogs.

Since the premises are true and the conclusion is false, and since this argument has the same logical structure as the argument we wish to analyze, we can safely conclude that the original argument is invalid, as is **any** argument of the same logical structure.

8.7. Important Syllogistic Forms

A **syllogism** is a deductive argument with two premises. Aristotle believed that all deductive arguments can be put into syllogistic form. While scholars do not all agree with this claim, it is undeniable that there are a few forms of the syllogism that occur again and again in actual argumentative discourse and therefore merit knowing well. We will look at four *valid* forms of the syllogism and two *invalid* forms.

8.7.1. *Modus Ponens*

$P \rightarrow Q$
P
______
Q

This argument form is valid. That is, if any proposition Q follows from any proposition P, and if proposition P is asserted as true, it logically or necessarily follows that Q must be true.

8.7.2. *Modus Tollens*

$P \rightarrow Q$
$\sim Q$
______
$\sim P$

This argument form is valid.

8.7.3. Hypothetical Syllogism

$$\frac{P \rightarrow Q \qquad Q \rightarrow R}{P \rightarrow R}$$

This argument form is valid.

8.7.4. Disjunctive Syllogism

$$\frac{P \vee Q \qquad {\sim}P}{Q} \quad \text{or} \quad \frac{P \vee Q \qquad {\sim}Q}{P}$$

This argument form is valid.

The following two argument forms are *invalid*. They are useful to know because they so closely resemble modus ponens and modus tollens, respectively, that people frequently express these argument forms thinking them to be valid.

8.7.5. Affirming the Consequent

$$\frac{P \rightarrow Q \qquad Q}{P}$$

This might look like a good argument at first glance, but consider the following example:

If it rains, the street gets wet.
The street is wet.
———————————
Thus, it must have rained.

What is wrong with this argument is that streets can get wet from means other than rain: street cleaners and overturned trucks, for example.

8.7.6. Denying the Antecedent

$$\frac{P \rightarrow Q \qquad {\sim}P}{{\sim}Q}$$

Again, consider our wet street example: If it rains, then the streets get wet. It is not raining. Therefore, the street must be dry (not-wet). Again, what if the street cleaner had just been here?

CHAPTER 9

Informal Logic

Now that we have seen how formal logic focuses upon and deals with the form of deductive arguments, hopefully we all have a better notion of **form** in arguments. For the rest of this text, we will be utilizing the techniques of informal logic, with an interest in both form and content questions. Since all the techniques of informal logic revolve around answering these two questions about each argument in question (in its context), it is important to recall these questions.

The form question: Does the conclusion **follow from** the premises?

The content question: Are the premises expressed or tacitly relied upon **true** or **acceptable**?

CHAPTER 10

Interpreting Arguments—Getting the Argument Straight

Perhaps the most crucial—and difficult—step in the logical analysis of arguments is the very first step: figuring out what argument has been presented. All subsequent analyses depend upon this first step. If the argument is not understood correctly, then the analysis of the argument may well commit the **straw man** fallacy (this is explained in section 14.11; basically, the straw man fallacy is committed when someone misrepresents his or her opponent's argument).

It is very important to avoid even the perception that you are misrepresenting someone's argument, for several reasons. First of all, it detracts from dialectic, as people tend naturally to get upset if they think that someone is not being fair to them (and often even if one is being unfair to another). We all hate to say or to have said to us: That's not what I said! (But think of how often we hear those words in argumentation.) Recall that our rhetorical strategies designed to **promote dialectic** include not incurring emotional reactions to arguments and interpretations of arguments. Anger dims attention to detail. Likewise, one's **ethos** is tarnished if one's audience thinks that one is misrepresenting an argument: if audience members think that you are intentionally misrepresenting the argument, they will doubt your integrity; and if they think that you are misrepresenting the argument due to ignorance or lack of attention, they will lose faith in your intelligence or seriousness about the issue. If any of these happens, you are on the rhetorical road to being ignored by your audience.

Here are some recommendations to help you get straight what an argument is saying:

1. Read (or listen to) each argument carefully. (Remember: Arguments are often very hard to interpret, for reasons that will be discussed further subsequently.)
2. Keep the context of the argument in mind.
3. Ask yourself what the issue is.
4. Identify the different positions that might be taken in the controversy.
5. Then ask yourself what the *point* of the argument is: this will be the conclusion of the argument.
6. Finally, ask what *reasons* or *evidences* are presented (or tacitly relied upon) to persuade you to accept the conclusion. These will be the premises of the argument.

7. Avoid the urge to rush in and critique an argument until you have done a thorough job of interpreting the argument.

> **Rules for interpreting arguments:**
>
> 1. **Read/listen carefully**.
> 2. Be aware of the **context**.
> 3. Be aware of the **issue**.
> 4. Identify different **positions** taken on the issue.
> 5. Find the **point** (conclusion) of the argument first.
> 6. Then find the **reasons** or **evidence** (premises) offered in the argument.
> 7. Avoid **premature critique**; first **get the argument straight**.

Remember that interpreting and analyzing arguments depend upon two parts: **form** (that is, for deductive arguments, *not, and, or, and if . . . , then . . .*) and **content** (key concepts and conceptual connections).

Because arguments are often subtle, it is a good practice to **write down** the logical structure of an argument before beginning your analysis. In order to clarify the logical structure (as opposed to the rhetorical structure) of arguments, put the argument into what is called **logical structure**. This is achieved by listing the premises in order, labeling them, and following them with the conclusion according to the following schema:[1]

P1: xxxxxxxx
P2: xxxxxxxx
P3: xxxxxxxx
———————
C: xxxxxxxx

Quite often, an argument will contain **subarguments** in the main argument. This occurs when one or more of the premises of the main argument are supported with reasons or evidence. This is often done right after a main premise is mentioned. Consider the following argument:

> If we lower taxes, inflation will rise. When people have more pocket money, they will spend it. We don't want higher inflation, so we shouldn't lower taxes.

Let's put this into logical structure: in doing so, we will point out the subargument by a notational convention:

    P1A: When people have more pocket money, they will spend it.
P1: If we lower taxes, inflation will rise.
P2: We should not cause inflation.
———————
C: Therefore, we shouldn't lower taxes.

[1]The basic form of the logical structure employed in this text is adapted from Ralph Johnson and J. Anthony Blair, *Logical Self-Defense* (New York: McGraw-Hill Ryerson, 1977).

Note that by indenting the first claim and labeling it *P1A*, we clearly set it out as contributing to P1: P1 can thus be seen to be a conclusion of an argument with one premise P1A. Note further that the argument as represented in logical structure has changed the **order** of the statements labeled *P1A* and *P1*. This change of order is important. Arguments are generally produced in order to persuade people to accept a conclusion. As such, they can be said to be delivered according to a **rhetorical structure.** For instance, in the preceding argument, P1 was introduced to persuade the listener to accept the conclusion. Once P1 was introduced, however, the arguer wanted to "drive the point home" with further reasoning and thus followed up P1 with P1A. Here, P1A→P1 is a **subargument**, P1A being the premise and P1 being the conclusion of the subargument. This is a common form of argument: a major premise is stated followed by the reason(s) for accepting it. Thus, the **rhetorical structure** (the order for presenting claims to audiences) of arguments often begins with the conclusion and then presents the premises supporting it. When placing arguments into logical structure, we wish to display the **logical structure** of the claims. There is good reason to do this: it is much easier to **assess** arguments if they are presented in logical order. That is, it's easier to spot good and bad forms of inference when the premises are presented first followed by the conclusion (including the premises and conclusions of subarguments like P1A→P1 in the example). Later, we will learn a few more notational conventions that are designed to clarify the logical structure of arguments.

> The **rhetorical structure** of an argument is simply the argument, as it is presented by the arguer.
>
> The **logical structure** of an argument is a diagram that displays the logical structure of the argument (all displayed according to logical features, including the stated and unstated portions).

10.1. Unstated Premises

Unstated premises are premises (grounds or warrants—these terms are defined later; for now, see the glossary) or conclusions that are unstated but that an argument relies upon if it is to be valid (or strong, in induction). For instance, consider the argument:

P1: Joe killed a defenseless and innocent little old lady.
___
C: Therefore, Joe is immoral.

This argument is invalid as stated. That is, the conclusion does not follow necessarily from the premises. An important term, *immoral*, appears in the predicate of the conclusion, yet it appears nowhere in the argument's premises (recall here from the box describing deduction and induction in section 6 that the conclusion is "contained in" the premises of a valid argument). However, once this is noticed, an obvious tacit warrant comes to mind that, when added to the argument, makes it valid (again, *W* here means *warrant*, to be explained subsequently; for now, see the glossary):

UP2(W): All killing of defenseless and innocent little old ladies is immoral.

It seems likely that this premise was implied by the arguer (and may be accepted by the arguer's target audience). It is labeled "**UP**" to note that it is an **unstated premise**, unstated but relied upon by the argument. Many—in fact, most—arguments in real life rely upon important but unstated premises, which we all tend to "fill in" in our understanding of the arguments, based upon their context. One important reason for diagramming the logical structure of arguments is to make us more aware of such unstated but necessary parts of arguments; becoming aware of them makes both the form and the content of arguments more clear. As we will see, it is often necessary to discuss or challenge unstated assumptions in arguments.

Note that several other premises could have been added to make this argument valid. Instead of UP2, we might have introduced either of the following:

UP3(W): All killing is immoral.

UP4(W): Killing old ladies is immoral.

Both of these make the argument valid. If all killing—or just the killing of old ladies—is immoral, then it follows that the killing of a defenseless and innocent little old lady is immoral. The reason for choosing to assert UP2 rather than UP3 or UP4 is that it is a **weaker claim** than the other two. Many people who believe the killing of defenseless and innocent little old ladies is immoral do not believe that all killing—or even all killing of old ladies—is immoral. These people hold that—in cases of war, execution, and self-defense—a morally acceptable killing may indeed occur.

Thus, according to the **principle of charity**, in filling in UPs one must avoid attributing to the author of an argument a **stronger claim** than the one required by the argument (as stated and in context). Otherwise, one runs the risk of committing what is called a *straw man* in section 14.11.

Rule of thumb: Add the *weakest* UPs that show the logical connection between the stated Ps and the stated/implied conclusion.

10.2. Rhetorical Implications

Rhetorical implications (RIs) are conclusions or premises that, although unstated, are directly implied (in context) by some statement that is made. Such uses of statements to imply others are often referred to as "tricks" because they trigger emotional rather than rational responses (and thus subvert dialectic). The conclusions or premises implied by such statements are quite often unacceptable or false. A partial classification of rhetorical implications includes: rhetorical questions, rhetorical commands, irony, and overstatement and understatement.

10.3. Rhetorical Questions

Rhetorical questions (RQs) are especially tricky. They can imply several claims at the same time. A popular form of the rhetorical question is to ask one's opponent in debate, "You don't really believe that, do you?" Note that this implies that the opponent must be either insincere or stupid (or perhaps both). In assessing or composing an argument, it is necessary to translate rhetorical questions into their hidden claims.

10.4. Rhetorical Commands

Rhetorical commands (RCs) such as "Let's all vote for Senator Snodgrass!" imply a kind of "peer group camaraderie" that makes people feel uncomfortable if they happen not to wish to vote for Senator Snodgrass.

10.5. Irony

Irony plays a pervasive role in argumentation. In irony, one says one thing while implying just the opposite. We are so used to seeing irony that we are generally adept at catching the true intent of ironic statements (TV sitcoms consist of about 80 percent irony). However, several problems arise when irony is used in arguments, especially written ones. It is harder to catch irony as irony in written texts; whereas in spoken situations, irony is usually accompanied by some gesture or grimace to make its intent clear. Using irony in arguments can also backfire: if the target audience misses its ironic intent, it can think that the arguer is arguing for the opposite side. Also, in our goal to control our rhetoric to promote dialectic in argumentation, we must be aware that irony can anger or alienate our audience, as it may be taken as "talking down" to our target audience.

10.6. Overstatement and Understatement

Overstatement and **understatement,** like irony, imply something other than they actually say. For instance, in a political campaign characterized by a lot of mudslinging, a politician might say, "My worthy opponent would *never* stoop to mudslinging," or "My worthy opponent *always* sticks to the issues." Overstatement and understatement run the same risks as does irony in arguments. It is best to say exactly what you mean in arguments, to promote dialectic and clarity.

In analyzing the arguments of others, rhetorical implications, questions, and orders, as well as irony and understatement and overstatement, should all be noted as such when putting arguments into logical structure. To put them into the logical structure, you should write out the proposition(s) you think the arguer is really implying, rather than what the arguer says, and then label those premises accordingly. For example, consider the following argument:

> Why doesn't Senator Scratch see the folly of his ways? His support of higher welfare payments will lead our great nation into financial disaster. The cases of welfare fraud reported this week are a further example of the insanity of welfare payments. Let's all vote for Scratch's opponent for senator!

To put this into logical structure:

P1(RQ): Senator Scratch's policy on welfare is folly.
P2A: Cases of "welfare fraud" were reported this week.
P2B(RI): These cases (P2A) are typical or representative of what happens when welfare payments are available.
UP2C(W): Many fraudulent welfare claims will lead to financial disaster.
P2: [Senator Scratch's] support of higher welfare payments will lead our great nation into financial disaster.
P3(RI): Welfare payments are insane.
UP4(W): We should avoid policies that are disastrous or insane.

C(RC): Voters should vote for Scratch's opponent for senator.

Note how the labeling of RQs, RIs, and RCs **promotes dialectic**: by restating the rhetorical expressions as **implied propositions** and **labeling** them as our reformulations, we bring out the "hidden" claims imbedded in the argument, while at the same time noting that we admit to having **interpreted** these claims. Now it is open to the author of the argument to "save face" by objecting that we have misrepresented his or her argument. Should this occur, we can "take back" the interpretations and ask the author to state his or her position more clearly. If the author is not available, we have still avoided charges of committing a **straw man** (misrepresenting an argument or position) at least to the extent that we have noted where our wording differs significantly from the author's and also noted why we think our wording is required (because the author's language seems to us to contain "hidden implications"). The use of these labels, like the use of UPs and UCs, makes the logical structure of the argument clearer. It also helps to keep all claims and evidence "open and above board," the better to **promote dialectic**.

Furthermore, note that we have replaced the pronoun "His" in P2 with "[Senator Scratch's]." This technique helps to clarify the argument and is especially useful when sentences are rearranged to exhibit logical structure. If several persons are mentioned in an argument, and it is necessary to keep them separated, the use of their initials or names every place they are mentioned may be helpful. This is especially useful when the shift from the rhetorical to the logical structure of the argument moves sentences around quite a bit.

These rules for putting arguments into logical structure should not be treated as absolutes; as you tackle a number of different arguments, you might find further useful techniques. The purpose is to make the argument form clear. Use whatever means necessary to **promote dialectic**.

> **Rhetorical strategy:** In general, avoid RQs, RCs, and RIs, irony, and overstatement and understatement, since these strategies often "backfire" and undermine your **ethos**.

10.7. The Toulmin Model

Another helpful form for representing argument structure is called the **Toulmin Model**. This model has been adapted from a book coauthored by Stephen Toulmin[2] but has here been modified using

[2]Steven Toulmin, Richard Riecke, and Allan Janik, *An Introduction to Reasoning,* 2nd ed (New York: Macmillan, 1984).

certain features of the logical structure. The Toulmin Model provides a somewhat different—and very useful—framework for analyzing and assessing arguments. Like the logical structure, the framework provided by the Toulmin Model displays the **structure** or **relationship** that exists—or, at least, should exist—between the propositions of an argument that purports to be rationally persuasive. As such, the Toulmin Model may be used as a "heuristic" in composing and interpreting arguments. The Toulmin Model is "heuristic" in the sense that the application of the Toulmin Model permits more than one specific analysis of the structure of an argument. Here, we use only a portion of the Toulmin Model.

Before explaining the Toulmin Model, let us look again at the nature of arguments. People argue in order to persuade each other to accept, believe, or do something. Recall that **argumentation** is the living process in which people exchange insights, reasons, and points of view in order to persuade; whereas **arguments** are the written or spoken texts that people present to each other in order to persuade them. Thus, an argument is a text abstracted from the living process of argumentation. In approaching and interpreting arguments, it is extremely important to remember their context in argumentation, the use to which they are put. This is a major factor in controlling polysemy (see section 3.1.1) in argumentation. To see how the Toulmin Model works, let us now examine four simple one-sentence arguments:

1. There's smoke coming out of that house, so it must be on fire.
2. He killed an innocent old woman, so he should be punished to the full extent of the law.
3. He ate the leaves of a tomato plant, so he must see a doctor.
4. Every little boy gets dirty, and Tom's a little boy, so you know what to expect.

Like all arguments, each of the preceding examples has a point or **conclusion** (C) that the arguer is trying to get across or persuade the reader to believe.[3] In each of the preceding arguments, the claim is introduced by the word *so*:

C1: That house must be on fire.

C2: He should be punished to the full extent of the law.

C3: He must see a doctor.

C4: You know what to expect.

The claims in arguments 1 through 3 are straightforward enough, but the claim in argument 4 is really left unstated: the arguer clearly thought that his audience would "fill in" the proper **rhetorically implied conclusion** C(RI):

C(RI): Tom will get dirty.

It is not uncommon for arguers to leave the claim or conclusion to be filled in by their audience. In fact, this can be a rhetorically effective strategy of argumentation, since it forces the audience

[3]The Toulmin Model uses the term *claim* for what we call *conclusion* in this text. We will use the term *conclusion,* since both premises and conclusions are, in a rather straightforward sense, claims.

members to think of the claim on their own. (Teachers rely upon this technique a great deal, since it has been demonstrated that students do better at recalling information that they arrived at themselves, as opposed to being told the information.)

In addition to a conclusion, each of the preceding arguments presents a reason or a bit of evidence, which is supposed to persuade or convince the reader to accept the conclusion. In the Toulmin Model, the principal evidences upon which conclusions are based are called **grounds** (Gs). These sentences will spell out the facts, rules, some moral judgments, definitions, and so on, which the argument provides to support its conclusion. In our simple example arguments, these grounds seem clear:

G1: There's smoke coming out of the house.

G2: He killed an innocent old woman.

G3: He ate the leaves of a tomato plant.

G4: Tom's a little boy.

Grounds alone don't lead to a conclusion: the same facts, definitions, and so on may be taken and used in different ways to arrive at different conclusions. Thus, one or more **warrants** (W) are required to tie together the grounds and the conclusion. Warrants are most often left unstated (U). Let us use our examples to help explain the relationship between grounds, warrants, and conclusions.

In argument 1, only the conclusion and ground are stated:

G: There's smoke coming out of the house.

C: The house is on fire.

The connection between this ground and conclusion is, however, pretty clear. In fact, it is so obvious that the arguer left the warrant (W), which connects the stated ground to the conclusion, unstated:

UW: Where there's smoke there's fire.

This warrant is an inductively established "sign" statement: smoke is a sign of fire. Now consider the second argument: He killed an innocent old woman, so he should be punished to the full extent of the law. Again, the ground and the conclusion are clear:

G: He killed an innocent old woman.

C: He should be punished to the full extent of the law.

Here again, the warrant, the connection between the ground and the conclusion, was probably thought to be too obvious to be worth stating:

UW: One who kills innocent old women should be punished to the full extent of the law.

This warrant is a general moral or legal rule or principle that is applied to the particular case cited as the ground.

The third argument is perhaps less clear: He ate the leaves of a tomato plant, so he must see a doctor. The ground and the conclusion are hinted at through the word *so*, which seems to indicate reasons or grounds:

> G: He ate the leaves of a tomato plant.
>
> C: He must see a doctor.

The problem here might be summed up in the question "What is the connection between tomato leaves and doctors?" Here, an unstated warrant plus a further ground seem required:

> UG: Tomato leaves are poisonous.
>
> UW: One must see a doctor when poisoned.

These statements clarify the relation of the stated ground to the argument's conclusion.

The fourth argument is somewhat different: Every little boy gets dirty, and Tom's a little boy, so you know what to expect. This argument rhetorically implies its conclusion and states its ground but also states the warrant connecting them:

> G: Tom's a little boy.
>
> W: Every little boy gets dirty.
>
> C(RI): Tom will get dirty.

Thus, we have seen that the warrant (W) provides the **connection** between the G and the C by showing the relevance and propriety of moving from the set of assertions in the G to the assertion of the C. This is perhaps the most useful (if somewhat elusive) feature of the Toulmin Model, since all too many arguers seem to think that facts alone (Gs) dictate conclusions (Cs). The warrant of the Toulmin Model displays the need to "tie" these facts to the C.

In diagram form, the Toulmin Model looks like the diagram in figure 8 (including only the parts of the model that we will pursue in this text).

Rather than using Toulmin's diagram as our model, we will present arguments in logical structure and label the assertions of an argument under the headings of C, G, W, as was done in the preceding discussion. In fact, since all premises are G's or W's, we need use only one of these symbols; because of their importance, from now on we will label only the premises that are warrants (W), and it is assumed that the other premises are Grounds.

In addressing an argument in order to explain it, keep in mind the Toulmin Model's three categories of argumentative assertions: conclusion, warrant, and grounds. Familiarity with these

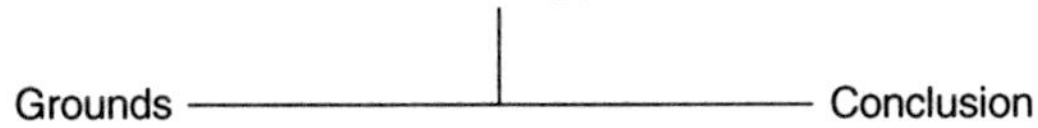

Figure 8: Diagram of the Toulmin Model

categories helps one to analyze the argument by providing a preliminary classification of its statements.

Now let us use the Toulmin Model's categories to analyze a more complex argument. The following argument is an editorial taken from the *New York Times* dated September 9, 1984. The paragraphs have been numbered for ease of reference.

Headline: Oh So Sure They're Right[4]

(1) This is what President Reagan said to a prayer breakfast in Dallas last month: People who resist the imposition of prayer in public schools are "attacking religion" and frustrating the will "of the great majority of Americans."

(2) This is what he said to a B'nai B'rith convention in Washington last week: the Constitution "makes sure that every single American is free to choose and practice his or her religious beliefs or to choose no religion at all. Their rights shall not be questioned or violated by the state."

(3) There is a contradiction here, evident to those who in fact choose no religion at all plus many Catholics, Jews, Protestants of varying persuasion, and others. What would Mr. Reagan advise them to do when their children are ridiculed for not participating in "voluntary" school prayers? Does he, truly, think they are free to go out and resist such religious practice? Or does he think, as he said in Dallas, that if they do resist, it is *they* who are guilty of intolerance?

(4) Intolerance: that is the word that is burning beneath all the smoke about religion and politics, a coupling that offends neither church nor state. There is plenty of religion in politics—and ought to be. People in a democracy should act on their social values, whether derived from their religious faith or from secular sources.

(5) Churches have long preached the social gospel. They have been prominent in the civil rights movement, in the Vietnam resistance, in antinuclear campaigns, even in partisan campaigns like the Rev. Jesse Jackson's run for the Democratic nomination. It is no sacrilege against the Constitution that, in place of the social gospel, other churches now preach Social Darwinism, inveigh on behalf of spending federal billions for new weapons and against spending any federal dollars for abortion.

(6) The danger comes from people who are oh so sure they're right, who insist that they alone represent the one, true, political faith, who revile the other side as godless, intolerant obstructionists.

(7) The president has come close to expressing just such certitude. Even though he seemed to moderate his views. Thursday before the B'nai B'rith, just two days before, to the American Legion, he was still dividing the world into children of light and children of darkness: "What some would do is to twist the concept of freedom of religion to mean 'freedom against religion.'"

(8) Religionists have every right to lobby for causes, to run for office, to criticize with vehemence—but not to misrepresent their opponents or ridicule their motives. Indeed, these rights carry with them a responsibility to respect other views. In short,

[4]I owe a debt of thanks to the Research Assistant Renee Clark who supplied this example argument.

tolerance: the vital insulator of democracy, the cushion that softens the sharp collisions between different views and faiths and enables all Americans to live together in reasonable harmony.

(9) Mr. A may strongly support capital punishment yet feel passionately that abortion is murder. Mrs. B may disagree with equal passion on both counts and demand of Mr. A, "Death is death. Why can't you see the inconsistency in your positions?" There are times when devout practitioners of one creed, though completely sure they are right, confront equally tenacious believers of the opposite. In this free society, the practical, not to mention moral, mechanism is tolerance.

(10) Did it ever occur to the president that opponents of school prayer might have worthy motives and are not out to frustrate "the great majority of Americans"? Did it ever occur to him that they might be right? And even if not, did it ever occur to him that their views deserve the president's **respect**?

(11) That would be tolerance. Or, as Learned Hand, the legendary jurist, said during the dark days of World War II: "The spirit of liberty is the spirit that's not too sure it's right."*

The point or **conclusion** of this argument seems to be stated at the start of paragraph 7:

C: The President has come close to expressing just such certitude.

The phrase "just such certitude" is not terribly clear when thus pulled out of context. We will use square brackets to explain what the phrase means, rather than says, by tying it to key concepts introduced in paragraphs 4 and 6:

C: The President has come close to expressing [a dangerously intolerant] certitude [which is a threat to freedom in America].

The editorial does not accuse Reagan of dangerous intolerance, but argues that his various speeches, when combined, seem to "come close to" such intolerance. Since this argument's conclusion is an **interpretation** of the point of view behind various speeches, it is quite proper so to qualify the conclusion. This strategy of argumentation is **dialectically effective** (that is, it contributes to a cooperative attempt to reach a mutually acceptable solution), in that it expresses a difference of opinion in such a way that its conclusions are limited, nonaccusative, and leave the opposition room to reply. (This particular qualification is especially important given the line of argument here; the argument would border on self-contradiction if the author were to take an intolerant position.)

The **grounds** which this argument offers to support its conclusion seem to be the following:

G1: President Reagan has contradicted himself in two speeches. [paragraph 3 supported by paragraphs 1 and 2]

G2: Intolerance is the principal issue concerning the relation between religious and political points of view. [This seems to be implied by the first sentence in paragraph 4 and the last sentence in paragraph 9.]

G3: When addressing the American Legion, President Reagan divided the world into children of light and children of darkness. [supported by a quotation from the speech in paragraph 7]

G4: {It seems not to have occurred to President Reagan} that opponents of school prayer might have worthy motives and are not out to frustrate "the great majority of Americans." [This statement seems implied by the first rhetorical question in paragraph 10.]

G5: {It seems not to have occurred to President Reagan} that they (opponents of school prayer) might be right. [This statement seems implied by the second rhetorical question in paragraph 10.]

G6: {It seems not to have occurred to President Reagan} that the views {of opponents of school prayer} deserve respect. [This statement seems implied by the third rhetorical question in paragraph 10.]

G7: The danger {to a democracy} comes from people who are oh so sure they're right; who insist that they alone represent the one, true, political faith; who revile the other side as godless, intolerant obstructionists. [paragraph 6]

Given these grounds, how are we to arrive at the conclusion? There seem to be three major **warrants** presented in the argument:

W1: The rights to lobby for causes, to run for office, and to criticize with vehemence carry with them a responsibility to respect other views. [paragraph 8]

This first warrant is backed up by the following **subargument**:

(W1)UP1(G): Tolerance is the vital insulator of democracy, the cushion that softens the sharp collisions between different views and faiths and enables all Americans to live together in reasonable harmony. [paragraph 8]

This defense of the first warrant is in fact the ground of a subargument which has W1 as its conclusion. The obvious connecting warrant between (W1)UP1(G) and W1 is:

(W1)UP2(W): The rights of democratic citizenship carry with them the responsibility to preserve and protect democracy.

The second warrant for the main conclusion is:

W2: Tolerance is a practical as well as a moral mechanism essential, to a free society. [paragraph 9]

This warrant is supported by the whole of paragraph 9, which will be summarized as follows:

(W2)P1(G): People in fact often hold firmly to beliefs that conflict with one another.

This is once more the ground of a subargument which has W2 as its conclusion. This subargument seems to rely upon an unstated warrant plus an unstated ground:

(W2)UP2(G): The lack of tolerance can lead conflicting opinions to result in tyranny. [This is a further ground of the subargument.]

(W2)UP3(W): We should maintain democracy and avoid tyranny. [This is the warrant of the subargument.]

The final warrant is expressed in the last paragraph:

W3: "The spirit of liberty is the spirit that's not too sure it's right." [paragraph 11]

This warrant is backed by an appeal to the authority of the man who made the conclusion:

(W3)P1(G): Learned Hand the legendary jurist said W3. [paragraph 11]

(W3)UP2(W): Hand is such an authority on American law that his words should be heeded.

The above interpretation of this argument is not the only one possible, but it does seem plausible given the text of the argument.

The categories of the Toulmin Model were instrumental in **explaining** the roles of the various statements in the argument, which in turn led to an **understanding** of the argument. This understanding is evidenced in the preceding interpretation by the comments, interpolations, and filling in of unstated but seemingly implied statements that accompanied the explanation. This intertwining of **explanation** and **understanding** is an important feature of the process of interpretation and merits some discussion.

When we first read an argument, we already have *some* understanding of it (including the limiting case of insight—the insight that we do not yet understand what the text is saying). The work of **explaining** a text thus relies upon our first grasp of it in **preunderstanding** (see section 3.1.2). The background knowledge of the meanings of words, of cultural context, of controversy, of the genre of the text, and of the author and audience of a text is all brought to bear in explaining a text, in analyzing its features and structures. (All this background knowledge also admits of limiting cases, the most extreme form being the explanation of an ancient text in an unknown language and from a virtually unknown cultural context.) **Explanation** thus rests on the level of understanding that we have in our first encounter with a text. For instance, in explaining the preceding editorial, we were guided by such understandings as the meanings of its words, the genre of the editorial (argumentative writing—which influenced us to apply the Toulmin Model to the piece), and the cultural and political setting of contemporary American politics.

Recall that preunderstanding is challenged and changed by the encounter with a text. The particularities of the text alter the way we see its setting. This is because a text addresses its setting; it is based in the **rhetorical exigence** of a writer working with a problem or issue and addressing an audience. **Exigence** is, briefly, what moved the author to produce the argument.

Because of the **polysemy** of words, interpreting is a **holistic** and **recursive** process. The **holism** indicates that the meaning of a particular word in an argument is interpreted on the basis of both its relation to the other words in the text and the contextual interpretation of the text (its **genre**, rhetorical exigence, assumed purpose, factual knowledge of the world, and so on)—the whole context and text. The job of interpreting arguments is **recursive**, because one must go through an argument again and again, relying upon levels of understanding stemming from earlier analyses, in order to produce a really good interpretation of the argument.

Our preunderstanding may be overturned by our **recursive** explanation of the various features of a text. For instance, an editorial might turn out to be not an argument but an **epideictic** text, that is, a text celebrating a social occasion (one often encounters such editorials on the Fourth of July and at Christmas); or an argument that we at first take straightforwardly might, at a later stage of explanation, be reinterpreted as being ironic and thus implying or *meaning* the opposite of what it explicitly *says*.

Likewise, a particular explanation of a part of a text often needs to be reevaluated after reaching a new understanding of the text. For instance, if a new insight makes us decide that a sentence we had interpreted as the argument's conclusion is in fact support for an unstated conclusion, we must now reexplain the role of that sentence in the argument. (Is it ground or warrant?) This **recursive process** might be outlined as follows:

1. Read text carefully.
2. In reading, look for the "point" (the conclusion).
3. Read again and again to get a feel for the interrelation of the statements (in terms of the categories of the Toulmin Model) and the relation between argument and subargument.
4. Use surface clues such as *since, for, because*, and so on, which usually introduce grounds or subarguments; and *thus, therefore*, and so on, which introduce conclusions (including the conclusions of subarguments, which may be grounds or warrants of the main argument).
5. Once you have a plausible interpretation of the surface structures of the text, look for **unstated** conclusions that may be required for the argument to be rationally persuasive—this must be done because arguers must assume some common (and thus left tacit) ground with the audience.
6. Now you are ready to assess the argument (find fallacies, good points, and so on), seeking fuller understanding.
7. After assessing the argument, reassess your interpretation by rereading the text, grounding each of your assertions in the surface features of the text—keeping in mind the **context** of argumentation in which the argument appeared (or is to appear).
8. Repeat steps 1 through 7 until you are satisfied with your interpretation of the argument.

The Toulmin Model also may be helpful in *composing* arguments. If you think through an argument you wish to write in terms of the Toulmin Model, you can develop a powerful framework for your argument. Developing your **conclusion** (which often shifts as you go through the recursive process of interpretation of your and other arguments) focuses you upon an issue or controversy and the variety of opinions held by others. Knowing that you must provide **grounds** will often send you to the library to gather facts and other evidence. Searching for a **warrant**, a convincing way of explaining the relevance and propriety of the grounds as sufficient to ensure acceptance of your conclusion by a particular audience, focuses your attention on the connections between your conclusion and the sorts of grounds that will be persuasive. Thinking about when and where **subarguments** for grounds and warrants are needed helps to make sure that you keep in mind the **audience** you intend to persuade, which in turn will force you to face actual or possible opposing warrants and grounds and different interpretations of the relationships between relevant grounds and conclusions.

This process of reading and writing using the Toulmin Model is also recursive. As you read relevant arguments and information, you should jot down notes. When you use the model to get ideas for your argument, you should take more notes. Drafting sections of the argumentative essay is often interspersed with further research on the issue. This process often changes the conclusion. Most often, this change is a gradual limiting of the original conclusion to limit it to available evidence. However, sometimes a complete change of face will occur, because finding more information about a topic may unearth convincing evidence and arguments for taking another view of the issue.

10.7.1. Finding the Warrants with GASCAP

More often than not, people leave their warrants unstated in arguments. In one sense, there is good reason for this: since warrants provide the connection between grounds and conclusions, we often expect this connection to be so obvious as to be not worth mentioning. Unfortunately, this leads to many misinterpretations. Therefore, in interpreting arguments, we quite often find ourselves looking for unstated premises that are warrants. Fortunately, there is an easy-to-remember acronym that can help us to find these warrants: GASCAP.[5] This acronym uses the first letter of the six most often used types of warrants:

Generalization: Generalizations use cited cases to generalize or predict to other cases.

Analogy: Analogies note similarities between two things or events and then draw further conclusions based on their similarity.

Sign: Signs are indicators. Smoke is a sign of fire—but not every smoke comes from fire (think of dry ice).

Cause: Causes are universal laws that govern the physical interaction of things in nature.

Authority: Authorities are persons especially knowledgeable in some field or event or such. We rely upon their testimony when we don't fully understand matters ourselves.

Principle: Principles are rules or maxims. They may be moral, religious, legal, or prudential.

[5] I owe this useful heuristic to my late colleague and friend Charles Kneupper.

In describing the application of the Toulmin Model to interpreting arguments, attention to **audience** has often been mentioned in the preceding sections. Attention to audience is crucial to persuasive argumentation. As an audience shifts (say, from a panel of experts on a topic to a general audience or to an audience of first graders), the same assertions often must be made in different words and phrasings. Furthermore, the need to provide grounds, warrants, and subarguments—and even to modify your own conclusion—will often shift when you address the same (or a related) line of argument to different audiences. For instance, consider an argument for or against capital punishment as presented to: a group of lawyers, to a police academy, and to a general audience. Knowing that each of these audiences has a different set of values, knowledge, and related beliefs could well cause you to emphasize different grounds, conclusions, and warrants for each group. A warrant that is common knowledge to lawyers may be wholly unknown to a general audience, thus requiring subarguments for the latter audience but not for the former. A ground such as "Capital punishment has not been shown unequivocally to deter crime" may well be accepted by a group of lawyers and yet be rejected by the members of a police academy. Thus, in composing arguments (as with any other sort of text), you should keep firmly in mind the nature of your **target audience**.

10.8. Strategy for Argument Interpretation—The Process of Moving from Rhetorical Structure to Logical Structure

Interpreting an Argument

1. Find the conclusion by rereading the argument several times. Remember the *principle of plenitude*: the interpretation must account for the entire text. The conclusion is the organizing focus of the argument. If the sentences in the argument are not numbered, number them sequentially to make it easy to refer to each sentence.
2. Reread the argument several times, with the conclusion in mind, then ask of *each sentence*:
    - Is it a part of the *argument*, or is it part of a *rhetorical move* (such as setting the focus of the issue, explaining exigence, or establishing ethos)?
        - If it is part of a rhetorical move, set it aside for now and look at the next sentence.
        - If you judge it to be part of the argument, ask if it is offered in evidence to support the conclusion or to support another sentence (that is, is it a main premise or is it a premise in a subargument)?
3. As you decide about each sentence, make a rough *diagram*, a "blocking out" of the logical structure of the argument by writing down the numbers of the sentences in a diagram of the logical structure (putting the conclusion at the bottom with a line over it; indenting subarguments to display the relations between main premises and

subarguments). Leave vertical space between each line in your diagram, to make it easy to insert unstated premises later. For example:

P1: #2

P2A: #4

P2B: #5

P2: #3
______
C: #1

4. When you have finished diagramming every sentence that is part of the argument, go back over your diagram, carefully comparing it with the argument text. Now look for *unstated premises*. Remember that these provide logical links between the sentences that are presented in the argument. Since we are looking for logical links, keep the following in mind:
   - Always keep in mind the *context* of the argument in its ongoing, living *argumentation*. This provides a lot of help in finding unstated premises and conclusions.
   - *Circling* or *underlining* of main ideas in the sentences in the argument helps you to focus your attention on the *conceptual relations* that constitute the *form* of the argument. By circling key words and phrases (often subjects and/or predicates of the sentences in the argument), you help to focus your logical intuitions to make this logical structure explicit.
   - *Warrants* provide the logical links between grounds and conclusion, and they are left unstated more often than not. Warrants make conceptual connections explicit.
     - Use the *GASCAP* acronym to help you find the warrants.
     - If the GASCAP method fails, try the "quick and dirty" method of finding warrants, which is based upon *modus ponens*:

       Modus ponens "quick and dirty" warrant finder:

       $P \rightarrow Q$ Unstated Warrant
       P Stated Ground
       ______
       Q Stated/unstated Conclusion

       —or—

       If (stated ground), **then** (stated/unstated) conclusion
   - Additional *grounds* that are needed for arguments (including subarguments) to "work" logically are often left unstated because arguers assume (sometimes correctly, sometimes incorrectly) that they are so obvious that they don't need to be mentioned.
5. After this process is finished, go over the text of the argument several more times, comparing it with your diagram of its logical structure. Critically evaluate your own interpretation and ask yourself:
   - Have I used the *principle of charity* to be fair to the implied logic of the argument?
   - Have I followed the *principle of plenitude* by accounting for the whole text of the argument?

- Have I followed the *principle of consistency* by not introducing any inconsistencies into the argument (unless I believe that the argument really is inconsistent)?
- Have I avoided committing the *straw man* fallacy by being fair in my interpretation and by clearly noting any changes I made to the text (such as bracketing interpolations; changing pronouns to nouns for added clarity; and using UPs, RIs, RQs, and RCs)?

6. Only after this entire process is finished are you ready to *critique* the argument.

Summary

1. Find *conclusion.*
2. Decide which sentences are *premises.*
3. Use diagram to distinguish *main premises* from *subargument premises, sub-subargument premises,* and so on.
4. Find *unstated premises.*
5. *Recheck* your analysis diagram, keeping in mind:
   - Principle of charity
   - Straw man fallacy
   - Changes and additions

10.9. Example Short Arguments for Interpretation and Analysis

This section contains eight sample arguments. The student is asked to diagram each argument, to create a logical structure for each one. The sentences in each of the following arguments have been numbered for ease of discussion and analysis later. The following section contains an analysis of each of the arguments.

The arguments presented with their analysis in section 10.10 are presented again in section 23.3 without their analysis as exercises to be done as homework and discussed in class. WARNING! Students are urged to resist the temptation to look at the sample analyses before attempting to diagram each of these arguments.

The first few times that one attempts to diagram an argument is a humbling experience: it is, to put it bluntly, very difficult. Using the sample analyses as a guide only *seems* to make the task easier. Providing such examples is dangerous, because students often think that the goal of this exercise is to diagram the argument just as the instructor did, but this is far from the case. Seeing examples as structures to be followed does not replace the very hard work of analyzing an argument carefully. The first attempts at argument analysis are almost always either incomplete or erroneous; we learn this critical thinking skill by making mistakes and being corrected.

I know from long experience as a teacher that most students are quite capable of learning how to do these logical structure diagrams; it just takes patience and hard work. But there is no substitute for the first, painful, humiliating encounter with the task. WITHOUT looking at the next section, please diagram each of the arguments in the exercises in sector 23.3, that is, create a logical structure diagram for each one. Do not attempt to critique the arguments; our natural urge to critique often keeps us from "getting the argument straight," from fully understanding what the argument is. We will address the elements of argument critique, in terms of the informal fallacies, later on in the text. The goal now is just to develop a clear understanding of the logical structure of an argument.

As a teacher, I often say at this stage of the course in critical thinking, "Logic is logic is logic." By this, I mean that the logic of each argument is not something subjective or personal. When we understand the logic of an argument, we can explain it to someone else, because logic is a rational structure of discourse. Of course, we need to pay careful attention to context in order to interpret the nuances of meaning in an argument, but the basic logical structure of an argument (we have seen many parts of this: premises, conclusions, warrants, subarguments, unstated but implied information, etc.) does not change from person to person, from place to place. Logical structure is in fact a very abstract part of human experience, as abstract and nonpersonal as arithmetic. In my experience, a typical class begins with a number of different interpretations of the logical structure of the same argument—but with practice, the students begin to produce more and more similar interpretations of the logic of an argument, because "logic is logic is logic." As students learn the nature of applied logic, their interpretations of arguments become more and more similar. Because of the large amount of unstated or implied information, there will always be differences between interpretations of the same argument; but there is remarkable unanimity on the basic logical structure of an argument, because logic is a structure that is built into the fabric of our thinking. We are emotional "naked apes," but we are also logical "rational animals." Logic is a structure of our lives and of our use of language. Like the basic structure of arithmetic, the basic structure of logic is everywhere; and, like arithmetic, we are almost all of us capable of figuring it out. Also like arithmetic, logic is hard to learn well; but with practice it can be a very useful skill.

10.10. Sample Argument Analyses

(1) (Background: This is adapted from a real advertisement, responding to the controversy over food additives—chemicals that are added to foods in processing to preserve, increase shelf life, etc.)

[NOTE: some of these sentences contain more than one claim, so these sentences have been split with slash marks (/), and suitable numbering has been added to make it easy to refer to the separate claims in diagramming and critiquing the argument.]

1. What's wrong with adding chemicals to our foods? 2. There is nothing unnatural about chemical food additives. 3. Everything in nature is made of chemicals. 4. Our bodies, /4.1 their cells, /4.2 the food we eat—all are made of chemicals. 5. Doctors know that /5.1 we need chemicals to grow and be healthy.

Logical Form

P1A1: #4
P1A2: #4.1
P1A3: #4.2
P1A: #3
P1: #2
P2A: #5
P2: #5.1

C: #1

P1A1(#4): Our bodies are made of chemicals.
P1A2(#4.1): Our cells are made of chemicals.
P1A3(#4.2): Our food is made of chemicals.
UP1A4(W-generalization): Thus by generalization:
P1A(#3): Everything in nature is made of chemicals.
UP1B(W-sign): If all of nature is made of chemicals, chemicals are not unnatural.
P1(#2): There is nothing unnatural about chemical food additives.
UP2(W-principle): If food additives are not unnatural, then there is nothing wrong with adding them to our foods.
P3A(#5): Doctors know that we need chemicals to grow and be healthy.
UP3B(RI or UP)(W-authority): Doctors are right about P2, because of their expertise.
P3(RI, #5.1): We need chemicals to grow and be healthy.
UP4(W-principle): There is nothing wrong with doing something that promotes healthy growth.

C(RQ, #1): There is nothing wrong with adding chemicals to our foods.

Assessment

Form: The argument is basically *deductive*, with inductive support for P1A. Although *valid* with unstated premises, because the conclusion follows necessarily from the premises, the warrants are highly questionable. The form is OK, but the warrants are fallacious.

Content:

P1A1 through P1A: all OK[6]
UP1B and P1: *ambiguity* on "natural," since many natural substances (e.g., snake venom) are harmful, and we would not want to add them to our foods. Because of this ambiguity, P2 is also *ambiguous* for the same reason.
UP3B: *improper appeal to authority* (authority unnamed)
P3: *ambiguity* on "chemicals"; not all chemicals promote healthy growth.

[6]Actually, from what we know of things like stars, atoms, etc., P1A is not true—but perhaps this charge of problematic premise would be somewhat picky, since in dealing with food additives we are dealing at the biological level.

(2) (Background: Spoken during a debate over smoking in public places)

1. Those nonsmokers should leave smokers alone. 2. Anyone who spends his time on nonsmokers' rights is ignoring more important matters. 3. To argue that nonsmokers have the right to clean air is to ignore the terrible pollution of our air by industry. 4. Smokers are just minding their own business, since /4.1 they are doing something that does not hurt anyone else.

Logical Form

        P1A: #3
P1: #2
        P2A: #4.1
P2: #4
___
C: #1

P1A(#3): To argue that nonsmokers have the right to clean air is to ignore the terrible pollution of our air by industry.
UP1B: Industrial air pollution is more important than smokers' pollution.
UP1C(W-sign): To focus on relatively unimportant issues is to ignore important issues.
P1(#2): Anyone who spends his time on nonsmokers' rights is ignoring more important matters.
UP2(W-principle): One should not concentrate on less important matters.
P3A(#4.1): [Smokers] are doing something that does not hurt anyone else.
UP2B(W-sign): Doing something that hurts no one is a sign of minding one's own business.
P3(#4): Smokers are just minding their own business.
UP4(W-principle): People who mind their own business should be left alone.
___
C(#1): Those nonsmokers should leave smokers alone.

Assessment

Form: The argument is *deductive*, because it is neither a generalization/prediction nor an argument by analogy. It is *valid* with the use of some relatively obvious, unstated warrants.

Content:

P1A: This is a *problematic premise*, because many address more than one problem. Also, it is a classic *red herring*, trying to switch the subject to industrial air pollution.
P1B and P1C: This is a *red herring*, because the arguer is trying to focus attention away from the current problem by calling attention to another problem.
P1: This is a *red herring* for the above reasons. It is also a *problematic premise*, because some people fight against both smokers' pollution and industrial pollution.
P2: This is both a *red herring*, since it changes the subject, and a *problematic premise*, in the sense that any problem deserves attention. The overall strategy is one of red herring.
P3A: This is a *problematic premise*, because there is clinical evidence to suggest, possibly prove, that "second-hand smoke" is injurious to nonsmokers.
P3: This is a *problematic premise*, since our collective health is a collective problem.
P2B and P4: In general these are true.

(3) (Background: Fictitious letter to the editor during a senatorial campaign)

1. Why would anyone want to vote for Senator Snodgrass? 2. His conduct has been bad for the Texas economy. 3. Why, I visited Washington and saw him sleeping during the debate on the supercollider. 4. The man votes like he sleeps through every debate. 5. He has flip-flopped on almost every issue on the docket.

Logical Form

<table>
<tr><td>
P1A1: #3
P1A2: #3.1
P1A(RI#3):
P1: #2
P2: #4
P3: #5
———————
C(RQ): #1
</td><td>OR</td><td>
P1A1: #3
P1A2: #3.1
P1A(RI#3)
P1B: #4
P1C: #5
P1: #2
———————
C(RQ): #1
</td></tr>
</table>

(1st version)

P1A1(#3): I visited Washington.
P1A2(#3.1): I saw Sen. Snodgrass sleeping during the debate on the supercollider.
UP1A3(W-authority): I am an eye witness.
P1A(RI, #3): [Sen. Snodgrass] slept during the debate on the supercollider.
UP1B: The supercollider was important for the Texas economy.
UP1C(W-cause or sign): Sleeping during an economically important vote is bad for the Texas economy.
P1(#2): [Sen. Snodgrass's] conduct has been bad for the Texas economy.
UP2(W-principle): You should not vote for a candidate who has been bad for the economy.
P3(#4): [Sen. Snodgrass] votes like he sleeps through every debate.
UP4(W-principle): You should not vote for a candidate who votes like he sleeps through every debate.
P5(#5): [Sen. Snodgrass] has flip-flopped on almost every issue on the docket.
UP6(W-principle): You should not vote for a candidate who flip-flops on most issues.
———————————————————————————
C(RQ, #1): You should not vote for Senator Snodgrass.

Assessment

Form: *Deductive*, because it is not a generalization or prediction from stated cases, or an argument by analogy. It is *valid* with obvious UPWs, because the conclusion follows necessarily from the premises.

Content:

P1A1 through P1A: OK; we accept the testimony of eyewitnesses, unless we suspect conflict of interest.
P1B, C: OK
P1: This is a *hasty generalization*, if it is meant as a *general* criticism based on *one* event in the subargument.

P2, P4, P6: OK

P3: This is a *problematic premise*, an overstatement without more evidence (more cases, for the same reason as P1). One could also cite the fallacy of *vagueness*, since it is not really clear what is meant by "votes like he sleeps through every debate"; that sounds suspiciously like a mere expression of disagreement, without further evidence.

P5: This may be acceptable, if the target audience is expected to know this from past press releases and debates; otherwise, it is probably a *hasty generalization*, for the same reason as P1.

(4) 1. If we raise taxes, it will be a disaster for the economy. 2. People will have less to spend, small businesses will fail, people will be without jobs, and this will shrink the tax base; so, raising taxes will actually lower revenues.

1. If we raise taxes, it will be a disaster for the economy. 2. People will have less to spend, /2.1 small businesses will fail, /2.2 people will be without jobs, and /2.3 this will shrink the tax base; so, /2.4 raising taxes will actually lower revenues.

Logical Form: [NOTE: the "if" in sentence #1 carries through the entire argument, which is hypothetical because taxes have not yet been raised. NOTE further the "logical chain" of the clauses, separated by commas, in sentence #2.]

P1A: #2
P1B: #2.1
P1C: #2.2
P1D: #2.3
P1: #2.4
____
C: #1

P1A(#2): If we raise taxes, then people will have less to spend.
P1B(#2.1): If people will have less to spend, then small businesses will fail.
P1C(#2.2): If small businesses will fail, then people will be without jobs.
P1D(#2.3-W-cause): If people will be without jobs, then this will shrink the tax base.
UP1E(Ground): Revenues come from the tax base.
P1(#2.4): If we raise taxes, it will actually lower revenues.
UP2(W-cause): If we lower tax revenues, it will be a disaster for the economy.
____
C(#1): If we raise taxes, it will be a disaster for the economy.

Assessment

Form: *Deductive*, because it is not a generalization/prediction from stated cases, or an argument by analogy. It is *valid* with obvious UPWs, because the conclusion follows necessarily from the premises.

Content:

P1A: This is a *questionable cause* or a *problematic premise*, because some economists, citing the law of marginal utility, argue that many of the poor will continue to spend the same (out of necessity); also some of the very rich will continue to spend.

P1B: This is a *questionable cause*, because small businesses could accommodate tax increases by laying off employees or raising prices. Business is a complex issue.

P1C: This is a *questionable cause*, because often people laid off can find other jobs.

P1D: This is a *questionable cause*, because of the different options open to individuals and businesses. After all, someone might think of a strategy that no one has thought of before.

P1E: OK; in this context revenues come directly from the tax base.

P1: This is a *problematic premise* and, because of the questionable causes in the subargument, this is a classic *slippery slope.*

P2: This is a *problematic premise*, because it assumes that cuts in spending could not offset deficits in funding.

(5) (Background: Spoken to a friend who is in the market for a new car)

1. You should buy the Speedo Supreme. 2. It is a fine automobile. 3. It is dependable, with the tried-and-true hydraulic suspension and an award-winning automatic transmission. 4. It is inexpensive to operate. 5. Why, in independent road tests it beat both the Ford and the Toyota for gas mileage. 6. It goes ten thousand miles without a change of oil, and is aerodynamically designed. 7. Furthermore, it comes with a super sound system.

Logical Form

P1A1: #3.1
P1A2: #3.2
P1A: #3
P1B1: #5
P1B2: #6
P1B3: #6.1
P1B: #4
P1C: #7
P1: #2

C: #1

P1A1(#3.1): [The Speedo Supreme] has the tried-and-true hydraulic suspension.

P1A2(#3.2): [The Speedo Supreme] has an award-winning automatic transmission.

UP1A3(W-sign): A tried-and-true hydraulic suspension and an award-winning transmission are signs of a dependable car.

P1A(#3): [The Speedo Supreme] is a dependable car.

P1B1(#5): In independent road tests [the Speedo Supreme] beat both the Ford and the Toyota for gas mileage.

P1B2(#6): [The Speedo Supreme] goes ten thousand miles without a change of oil.

P1B3(#6.1): [The Speedo Supreme] is aerodynamically designed.

UP1B4(W-sign): Good gas and oil mileage and aerodynamic design are signs of a car's being inexpensive to operate.

P1B(#4): [The Speedo Supreme] is inexpensive to operate.

P1C(#7): [The Speedo Supreme] has a super sound system.

UP1D(W-sign): Dependability, inexpensive operation, and super sound systems are signs of a fine car.

P1(#2): [The Speedo Supreme] is a fine automobile.

UP2(W-principle): You should purchase a fine automobile.

C(#1): You should buy the Speedo Supreme.

Assessment

Form: *Deductive*, because it is not a generalization/prediction from stated cases, or an argument by analogy. It is *invalid* (and thus *hasty conclusion*) in context, because to reach the conclusion one would also have to argue that there is no *other* car which is as fine as the Speedo Supreme. Buying a car is, after all, a matter of comparisons between competing makes and models, budgets, and so forth.

Content:

P1A1 through P1Ae: all OK

P1A: This is a *problematic premise*, because people argue the pros and cons of cars all the time; also *hasty conclusion*, because there are many other features that go into making a dependable car.

P1B1 through P1B4: all OK

P1B: This is a *problematic premise* and *hasty conclusion*, for the same reasons as P1A.

P1C, P1D: OK

P1: This is a *problematic premise*, for the same reasons as P1A, and *hasty conclusion*, because it does not take into consideration many factors that go into the decision to buy a car (budget, beauty, etc.).

P2: This may be a *problematic premise* for the same reasons as P1A.

(6) (Background: Spoken during a debate over whether or not to allow the sale of genetically altered fruit in grocery stores)

1. If we allow genetically altered fruit to be grown outside the laboratory, its spores can mix with the spores of other plants, both wild and domesticated. 2. When plants cross-pollinate, it can produce new species with unforeseeable properties. 3. So we might be bringing about the very shortage of food that the genetically altered foods were made to prevent.

Logical Form

P1: #1

P2: #2

C: #3

OR

P1A: #1

P1B: #2

P1: #3

UC: (policy statement)

[NOTE: This argument is a **policy argument** about legal or social policy. The two versions above are both common and proper interpretations of such arguments. We may interpret the argument narrowly, as in the first version, or more broadly, as in the second version, in terms of the policy (to allow or not allow the growing of genetically altered fruit outside laboratories—in this case: We should not allow the sale of genetically altered fruit in grocery stores.). This discussion also applies to argument #4, above.]

(1st version)

P1(#1): If we allow genetically altered fruit to be grown outside the laboratory, its spores can mix with the spores of other plants, both wild and domesticated.

P2(#2): When plants cross-pollinate, it can produce new species with unforeseeable properties.

UP3(W-cause): Creating organisms with unforeseeable properties *might* cause a food shortage. [NOTE: the qualifier "might" is required because it is in #3.]

C(#3): So we might be bringing about the very shortage of food that the genetically altered foods were made to prevent.

(2nd version)

P1A(#1): If we allow genetically altered fruit to be grown outside the laboratory, its spores can mix with the spores of other plants, both wild and domesticated.

P1B(#2): When [NOTE: "when" here means "if"] plants cross-pollinate, it can produce new species with unforeseeable properties.

UP1C(W-cause): Creating organisms with unforeseeable properties *might* cause a food shortage. [NOTE: the qualifier "might" is required because it is in #3.]

P1(#3): [If we allow genetically altered fruit to be grown outside the laboratory], we might be bringing about the very shortage of food that the genetically altered foods were made to prevent.

UP2(W-principle): We should not bring about a shortage of food.

UC: We should not allow the sale of genetically altered fruit in grocery stores. [NOTE: This is the policy conclusion.]

Assessment (of 1st version)

Form: *Deductive*, because it is not a generalization/prediction from stated cases, or an argument by analogy. It is *valid* with an obvious UPW, because the conclusion follows necessarily from the premises.

Content:

P1: This is a *problematic premise*, unless we think that the target audience already understands enough biology and genetics to believe that this is true. (A similar claim was argued for in an issue of *Scientific American;* so it might be true, but many would not know this.)

P2: This is a *problematic premise*, for the same reason as P1. [NOTE: the charges of *problematic premise* can shift when different audiences are involved, due to the concept of *acceptability*.]

P3: OK—Nature often surprises us!

(7) (Background: Spoken at a discussion of organic gardening)

1. Food additives should be banned. 2. Dumping chemicals in our food has affected the health of the entire nation. 3. Why, everyone knows that the incidence of cancer has increased ever since food additives have been placed into our diet.

Logical Form

P1A1: #3
P1A(RI): #3 w/o "everyone knows that"
P1: #2
___
C: #1

P1A1: Everyone knows that the incidence of cancer has increased ever since food additives have been placed into our diet.
UP1A2(W-authority): What everyone knows is true.
P1A(#3): The incidence of cancer has increased ever since food additives have been placed into our diet.
UP1B(W-cause): The rise of cancer is due to / caused by the presence of food additives in our diet.
P1(#2): Dumping chemicals in our food has (adversely) affected the health of the entire nation.
UP2(W-principle): We should avoid adversely affecting our health.
___
C(#1): Food additives should be banned.

Assessment

Form: *Deductive,* because it is not a generalization/prediction from stated cases, or an argument by analogy. It is *valid* with an obvious UPW, because the conclusion follows necessarily from the premises.

Content:

P1A1, P1A2: There is *ad populum* in "Everyone knows," because there is good reason to believe that not everyone knows this. [NOTE: Here you must supply the "good reason" noted above; sometimes "I didn't know this" will suffice—but of course someone else might ask, "Where have you *been*? Everyone knows this, don't they?"—and have a good point.]

P1A: Because of challenge to subargument, this may be called a *hasty conclusion.*

P1B: This is a *questionable cause* (*post hoc ergo propter hoc* or *complex cause*), because many other things happened at the time that food additives were being added to food. In fact, we know that "known carcinogens" have been added to the ground, air, and water in the same period. The affair of cancer is quite complex.

P1: This is a *hasty conclusion,* because of fallacies in the subargument, and *questionable classification* or *overstatement* ("entire"). It is also a questionable cause (*fallacy*) because many other factors are involved in the causes of cancer.

P2: OK

(8) (Background: Spoken in the University Center cafeteria)

1. College parking should be free and handy for students. 2. The students are the ones who need to get to class, so they should be allowed to park close to their classrooms. 3. After all, they are the ones who pay for all this. 4. The faculty, staff, and administration are working for the students, so they should be the ones to have to take buses from remote lots and pay for all the parking.

Logical Form

[NOTE: "close" (#2.1) and "handy" (#1) really say the same thing.]

    P1A: #2
P1: #2.1
P2: #3
    P3A: #4
P3: #4.1

C: #1, 2.1

    P1A(#2): The students are the ones who need to get to class.
    UP1B(W-principle): If the students are the ones who need to get to class, then they are the ones who should be allowed to park close to their classrooms.
P1(#2.1): [The students] should be allowed to park close to their classrooms.
P2(#3): [The students] are the ones who pay for [the university].
    P3A(#4): The faculty, staff, and administration are working for the students.
    UP3B(W-principle): If the faculty, staff, and administration are working for the students, then they should be the ones to have to take buses from remote lots and pay for all the parking.
P3(#4.1): [The faculty, staff, and administration] should be the ones to have to take buses from remote lots and pay for all the parking.
UP4(W-principle): If the faculty, staff, and administration should be the ones to have to take buses from remote lots and pay for all the parking, then college parking should be free and handy for students.

C(#1, 2.1): College parking should be free and handy for students.

[NOTE: the conclusion here really amounts to **two** separate claims. Thus the argument may be re-interpreted as in fact **two separate arguments**:

P1: #2
P2: #4

C: College parking should be handy for students.

and

P1: #3
P2: #4

C: College parking should be free for students.]

Assessment: (for 1st interpretation, taking it as one argument)

Form: *Deductive*, because it is not a generalization/prediction from stated cases, or an argument by analogy. It is *valid* with obvious UPWs, because the conclusion follows necessarily from the premises.

Content:

P1A: This is a *problematic premise*, because not only students, but faculty and staff also, need to get to class. One could argue, for instance, that in general faculty are older than students, and thus more in need of shorter walking distances to class. Also, staff often need equipment (vacuum cleaners, paint and buckets, etc.) to maintain the classrooms. This also makes P1 *problematic* (or a *hasty conclusion*) for the same reasons.

P2: This is a *problematic premise*, because not only students, but all taxpayers (including faculty, staff, and administration), support universities.

P3A: This is a *problematic premise*, because university employees in fact work for the state (in fact, for the country—some would argue, for humanity). This also makes P3 *problematic* (or a *hasty conclusion*), for the same reasons.

P4–P6: P4: This is acceptable, since the real problems with it were raised in the challenges to P1–P3. Remember that the goal in assessment is NOT to attack everything your opponent says, but to point out the (main) problems with their argument.

CHAPTER 11

Assessing Arguments—Form and Content

There are two main ways to test the acceptability of an argument:

1. **FORM:** Assess its validity (if it is deductive) or its strength (if it is inductive).
2. **CONTENT:** Ascertain whether or not its premises are true, or at least acceptable to the argument's audience.

All forms of logical analysis of argumentation are virtually contained in these two steps. As we saw in section 8, the logical structure of deductive arguments is determined almost completely by the concepts *not, and, or,* and *if. . . , then . . . .* The rest of argument form, when discussing informal logic (for which content as well as form is important), is supplied by **conceptual connections**. We evaluate an argument's content in the same way we evaluate the truth of any claim, appealing to empirical evidence, principles, definitions, and experience in general.

The testing of the truth or falsity of premises is often difficult; sometimes, we simply cannot be sure whether or not a premise is true. For this reason, it is useful to have a weaker test for premises. This test is **acceptability**. Premises in a controversy should be acceptable to rational and informed parties on **both sides** of the controversy. If you make conclusions in your premises that are acceptable only to those on "your side" of the argument, you will not rationally persuade others to your view. You will be left "preaching to the already converted," which does not promote dialectic, nor does it change minds. Keep in mind that your argument cannot be accepted unless each claim in it is accepted. (Recall our discussion of "boulders in a stream" in section 2.3.) The highest standard of acceptability is, of course, truth.

In composing arguments, the test for acceptability of premises requires judgment. There is no simple and universal rule for this (except perhaps: **be reasonable** and **know your target audience**). However, certain guidelines are helpful.

First, keep the **context** of the argument in mind. To what **target audience** is the argument presented? Technical information that is acceptable to a group of professionals will not be acceptable (without further explanation or argument) to a more general audience. Generalizations acceptable to a broad audience are often challenged by researchers in a specialized field. To be an effective dialectician, you must gauge your audience, choosing your points and your wording carefully to maximize clarity and communication; and this requires a control over your own rhetorical situation.

Another feature of the context of an argument is its place in an ongoing dialectic. How controversial are your claims? How crucial is each claim to your conclusion? It is not possible to argue for **every** claim you make, since each claim is backed by an argument that is itself made of claims, which would themselves have to be supported by argument—and so on, *ad infinitum*. However, the **burden of proof** usually falls upon whoever offers the argument, trying to persuade someone else of his or her viewpoint. Luckily, many claims made (or relied upon implicitly) in arguments are acceptable without proof simply because of the **context** in which the arguments appear. We all understand many things in common through culture and society. (This leads to interesting and thorny problems for those specialists who strive to interpret the language and culture of societies far removed in time or worldview.) Thus, one need not worry about explaining everything. It is often noted that a **principle of charity** is required in critical thought: don't be too picky, unreasonably requiring explanation for everything. Quite often, it is necessary to give an argument "a bit of slack," just to see where it will go. It is always best to assume that all parties in an argument are neither stupid nor evil, at least until ample evidence is in. One must, however, support with subarguments those claims that, in context, are judged reasonably to require further explanation. (Again, the target audience of the argument is a very important part of the context of argumentation.)

As a general rule, **the more controversial or important to your argument a claim is, the more argumentation and evidence are required to support it.**

Try to anticipate objections to your own argument. In constructing arguments, it is useful to mention likely objections and reply to them as a part of your argument (this is one form of subargument). This **promotes dialectic** by avoiding unnecessary discourse.

Cite the facts, research studies, and so on that support your conclusions. And be sure to note where experts disagree or when studies seem to support first one and then the other side of a controversy; in such cases, you will have to weaken your conclusion accordingly. Many arguments are weakened by the attempt to draw a strong conclusion when the available evidence simply won't support it. Admission of limitations of support for one's own view can lead to important (and useful) compromises. There is always time to gather more evidence to affect the compromise.

Deal with the issues that are either logically required by your argument or are often discussed in the controversy. If a related topic is debated again and again, show how it fits (or doesn't fit) into your argument.

Finally, always try to be open-minded, to integrate your argument into the wider contexts of the relevant issues and into life in general. Often, interesting new lines of argument arise when a perspicacious thinker sees a new correlation between some aspect of a controversy and other related issues.

To summarize the test for **acceptability**, we offer the following:

1. It is often a "call of judgment."
2. Consider your audience.
3. Support controversial conclusions.

4. Anticipate and reply to likely objections.
5. Cite support—and note where it is ambiguous (and weaken your conclusion accordingly).
6. Be open-minded.

However, even if all the premises of an argument are acceptable, still more is required: The premises must be **relevant** to the conclusion: and taken together, they must supply **enough evidence** to justify the conclusion.

Relevance is not always obvious (what is obviously relevant to an issue for one person is often seemingly irrelevant to another person), but one thing to watch out for is the overuse of the charge of irrelevancy. Quite often, people determine that evidence is irrelevant merely because they disagree with it or feel it threatens their view. Evidence is only irrelevant when it contributes nothing to the dialectic. If the relevance of a point is indirect, then the burden of proof is on the arguer to make clear its relevance to the issue and the argument.

The question of how much evidence is **enough evidence** is really another way of talking about validity (in deductive arguments) or strength (in inductive arguments). Once the premises have been tested for relevance and acceptability, one must still ask if there is **enough** evidence to entail the conclusion (or make it highly probable in the case of inductive arguments). The discussion of sufficiency raises an important issue: Quite often, arguments rely upon **unstated claims**, either premises or conclusions. These unstated conclusions may be divided into two general categories: **tacit implications**, which are left unstated, and **rhetorical implications**, which are stated or implied indirectly.

CHAPTER 12

Moral Arguments and Argumentation

Logic is a powerful tool. It can be used for good or for evil, to clarify or to confuse. While itself ethically neutral, it is difficult to avoid some discussion of ethics in setting out the **practical** use of logic. After all, one of the most important uses of argumentation is in trying to achieve ethical goals: we try to persuade others to adopt our ethical beliefs and practices. Is abortion a good practice? How about capital punishment? Logic helps us to sort out the many arguments on these and other important issues. While some hold strong beliefs on one side of such issues, others hold equally strong beliefs on the other side (and often there are more than two "sides" to an important issue). The fact that someone believes something is no rational reason for others to believe it. (After all, rational people once believed the world to be flat.) Let us examine the role of belief in argumentation.

12.1. Beliefs, Belief Systems, and Argumentation

Beliefs play a crucial role in the living process of argumentation. First of all, we generally argue about whether something or other should be believed or whether given our beliefs we should act in a certain way. Beliefs are thus in a sense a principal reason for arguing. Furthermore, we generally argue on the basis of evidence (premises) that we believe to be true for conclusions that we also believe to be true (or prudential) so that every statement in an argument might be prefaced with "I believe that . . . ." This is why it is not rationally persuasive to expect someone else to believe something just because you believe it; we argue about beliefs because people do hold *different beliefs*. Put another way, if we didn't already hold some different beliefs, we wouldn't be arguing. (We saw in section 2 that we couldn't argue if we didn't hold many beliefs in common.) However, the fact that arguments are usually about beliefs and based in beliefs is only one facet of the role of beliefs in argumentation.

"Belief" can also commonly mean "value." Beliefs in the sense of values also play a key role in argumentation. We wouldn't argue about factual beliefs or values if we didn't value interpersonal agreement of a particular sort. If you believed that the earth was flat, I wouldn't argue with you unless I valued our **sharing of beliefs and values**. If you believed in tyranny, I wouldn't argue with you unless I believed in some other political system—and unless I **cared** about our ability to share political beliefs. Social groups, whether political, religious, or educational, couldn't survive without shared values. (As Plato noted in his *Republic*, there must even be honor among thieves if a band of brigands is to survive as a band.) The process of argumentation is thus not only about and based in beliefs but also based in our need to share values and beliefs with others.

As we saw in section 2, the process of argumentation itself also requires some specific shared values. A commitment to **rational** persuasion requires a respect for the rights and rationality of one's opponent(s). We don't argue with infants, because they cannot understand us. We don't argue with soldiers or terrorists, because they have committed themselves to nonrational modes of persuasion. Thus, logic as a tool for the assessment of arguments and of the process of argumentation is closely tied to certain values concerning our fellow human beings. The ethics of the application of logical tools is the subject of the next subsection. However, first we must make one more point about the role of beliefs in argumentation.

The process of arguing about beliefs is made more difficult by the fact that beliefs, especially moral beliefs, form **belief systems**. Beliefs form systems in part because they may conflict. A look at two well-known (but rather vague) belief systems will make this clear. In arguments between "liberals" and "conservatives," one often hears accusations of hypocrisy or self-contradiction. A liberal might accuse a conservative of being self-contradictory for his or her opposing abortion while supporting capital punishment; and of course, the conservative can retort that the liberal is similarly self-contradictory for supporting legalized abortion while opposing capital punishment. But are liberals or conservatives necessarily contradicting themselves in espousing such views? Let us examine the situation

Issue	Liberal View	Conservative View
Abortion	Take life,	Save life.
Capital Punishment	Save life.	Take life.

When laid out this way, it seems indeed that both liberals and conservatives are contradicting themselves. However, what's missing from this analysis is a **sensitivity to context**. Let us fill in some information.

Issue	Liberal View	Conservative View
Abortion	"Take life" to preserve a high quality of life for those already living.	"Save life" because fetuses are innocent of any injustice and thereby deserve to live.
Capital Punishment	"Save life" to avoid errors and injustices.	"Take life" of capital criminals in order to preserve a high quality of life for the innocent.

Just this little bit of information (about warrants) makes the "obvious contradiction" of the two positions seem less obvious. Moral choices are often difficult because things valued by **both sides** in a debate conflict. Both liberals and conservatives believe, in general, in preserving innocent life, in maintaining a high quality of life (for the innocent), and in maintaining justice. It is in areas like abortion and capital punishment, where these values come into conflict with one another, that differing belief systems develop. Conflicts between such belief systems are extremely difficult to interpret and analyze, as is shown in chapter 13. For the time being, just keep in mind that because beliefs or values form systems, arguments over moral issues require a high degree of sensitivity to context.

The question is often *"Which is the lesser evil?"* One reason that moral arguments are difficult to conduct is that, when belief systems clash, people have sincere disagreements over which of several related evils is more important to avoid. When moral arguments proceed over a long time, it is usually because there are perceived evils from making certain decisions, no matter what side of the issue one takes. It is useful to remember this during moral arguments, as we tend to argue as if the other side were obviously evil and indefensible. If we recall that there are evils that result from either alternative in our action, it may help us to promote dialectic by being a bit more open-minded and charitable toward our opponents. After all, they believe that doing things our way will lead to morally unacceptable results, just as we believe the same of their choice.

12.2. Appeals to Rules and to Consequences in Moral Argumentation

Another reason that moral argumentation is difficult to sort out is that there are two radically different sorts of appeals made in evaluating situations, one basing moral decisions on rules, and one on consequences. Philosophers call these two sorts of appeals **deontological** and **utilitarian**, respectively.

Deontological concerns are appeals to the *intrinsic nature* of moral rules. For this reason, this sort of appeal is often characterized as **rule based.** The most famous example of a deontological philosopher is Immanuel Kant (1724–1804). Deontological systems of ethics assert that results or outcomes of our decisions are not our proper concern in ethical decision making, but that our attention should be directed to finding and following the proper moral rules. In many arguments, people appeal again and again to rules; they are arguing deontologically.

Utilitarian concerns are appeals to (possible) results or outcomes of actions. For this reason, this sort of appeal is often characterized as **outcome based**. We often try to anticipate the outcomes of our actions before we perform the acts themselves—this is generally accepted as an important part of moral reasoning. Some philosophers, such as John Stewart Mill (1806–1873), developed an ethical theory according to which outcomes are all-important in ethical decisions. They called their view "utilitarianism," and the basic aim of it was to **promote the greatest good for the greatest number of people**.

We need not go into the arguments philosophers have raised about the preferability of either of these views. What is important for our purposes is to recognize that in fact we often argue in *both* ways in moral argumentation; we appeal to rules, but we also appeal to the moral acceptability of the outcomes of decisions and actions. An imaginary example will help to make the difference between these two forms of moral reasoning clear.

As a **thought experiment**, imagine, if you will, that you are walking down a dark alley in Berlin in 1933. It is dark, and no one is near. You are musing, because you are an expert in politics and military technology. You are deeply worried because of the rise of a charismatic politician named Adolf Hitler, whom you expect to plunge Germany and the rest of the world into a devastating world war, a war that will claim hundreds of thousands, if not millions, of lives. You wish for some way to avoid this catastrophe. Then you pass a solitary figure seated on a crate in the alley. He seems not to notice you; he, too, is lost in thought. You take a few steps more, and then you realize that this man is none other than Hitler. You also remember that you have in your pocket a loaded gun. A thought flashes before your tortured mind: *I could kill him, I could prevent this terrible world war with one bullet.*

The moral dilemma here is, then, should you kill a fellow human being, who hasn't broken any law, or should you leave him be in spite of the disastrous consequences of his continued existence?

The deontologist's answer is clear: Murder is forbidden, no matter what. If we imagine Kant in the alley, we must imagine him sadly shaking his head and walking past Hitler. However, if we imagine J. S. Mill in the alley, we can imagine him turning suddenly, pulling out his gun, and firing, exclaiming, "I do this for the people of the world!"

The deontologist will not sanction the breaking of a moral rule on the basis of an imagined outcome (after all, we can never be certain that some other charismatic demigod will not take Hitler's place, possibly with even worse consequences). The utilitarian will feel very tempted to avoid the great suffering of the world's many by sacrificing one life.

This text will not attempt to tell you what should be done in such a situation; that is, after all, for us all to decide for ourselves in ongoing discussion. This is not the place to continue the argument between the rule-based and the consequence-based moral philosophies. It seems evident that people *do* reason and argue in both these ways in our everyday experience. Thus, we should recognize the difference between both forms of appeal and also appreciate the apparent acceptability of making both sorts of appeals. It seems senseless to ignore either rules or consequences in moral deliberations.

CHAPTER 13

Assessing Moral Arguments

Moral arguments present special problems for critical thinking. Because we all tend to care strongly about our moral choices and decisions, it is especially difficult to be self-critical about them. We often feel that our character is somehow at stake in moral arguments. Indeed, we must guard against the natural psychological tendency to regard mere **strength of belief** as strength of **reasonable evidence**. Belief is not a reason, for beliefs are often wrong. Reasons are evidenced or "evidence-able" beliefs. The reasonableness of a belief is a function of our ability to "give an account" of this belief, as Plato said long ago. Such an account must be rationally persuasive, not merely emotively persuasive. This should be kept in mind to help to keep our focus resolutely upon arguments and evidence, the better to **promote dialectic**. While much could be said about assessing moral arguments, we will focus upon a few rules of thumb that are useful for promoting dialectic in moral arguments. These rules of thumb concern unstated claims, facts and values, universal conclusions, and conflicting moral conclusions.

13.1. Unstated Claims

The argument about killing and punishment that we analyzed in section 10.1 exhibits a quite common structure encountered in moral arguments; it contained an unstated moral premise (UP2: All killing of defenseless and innocent old ladies is immoral). Remember that we all tend to think our moral reasons (premises) are shared by most everyone. This perfectly natural psychological fact results in the feeling that there is no need to state our moral rules and claims. As it turns out, however, people do disagree about moral matters. It therefore **promotes dialectic** to state the moral premises (in moral arguments, often moral warrants or warrants of principle) upon which an argument rests. Bringing out these claims makes us all more aware of what is at stake in moral disagreements. Above all, it helps us to see that there are often good moral grounds for more than one interpretation or point of view in moral matters. This promotes dialectic by avoiding the rather natural feeling that those who disagree with us on moral matters must be somehow evil or immoral.

Thus, as a **rule of thumb**, in moral arguments, be on guard for unstated moral premises (especially warrants). Also, always make your own moral beliefs and claims as clear as possible to others.

13.2. Facts and Values

Philosophers, in analyzing ethical arguments, often say: *You can't get an "ought" out of an "is."* What this means is, put in logical terms, that a moral conclusion requires a moral warrant. For example, consider the following argument.

> A fetus has a brain, arms, legs, hands, feet, a nose, ears, and a mouth. Thus, abortion should be illegal.

Let us put this argument into logical structure.

P1: A fetus has a brain.
P2: A fetus has arms.
P3: A fetus has legs.
P4: A fetus has hands.
P5: A fetus has feet.
P6: A fetus has a nose.
P7: A fetus has ears.
P8: A fetus has a mouth.
____
C: Therefore, abortion should be made illegal.

Notice that the conclusion of the argument is a moral conclusion (a value conclusion) signaled by the moral term *should* (other moral terms are *should not, ought,* and sometimes *must* and *must not*). But all the premises are factual statements. Why, after all, should the presence of a brain, legs, and so on in a fetus lead to the moral recommendation in the conclusion? The factual nature of the fetus is certainly **relevant** to our moral obligation either to permit or to prohibit abortion but it is hardly **sufficient,** in itself, to justify a moral decision about abortion. (For instance, rats have most of the listed physical qualities but very few would accept these facts as leading to the moral proscription of abortion of rats.) Thus, the preceding argument is tacitly relying upon a moral warrant that ties the relevant factual premises to the moral conclusion. Something like the following assumption is being made.

UP9: One should make illegal the killing of creatures with human features.

Notice further that this unstated moral warrant will likely be unacceptable to those who favor the legalization of abortion. Stating it seems to weaken the case against abortion. Actually moral arguments are often stated like this argument, because we all tend to find facts convincing. (After all, who wants to deny the facts of a case?) But the willingness to find a factual basis for our conclusions shouldn't blind us to the need for moral support for moral conclusions. Bringing out the moral warrant in moral arguments can help to clarify the issues at stake.

Thus, as a **rule of thumb,** an argument with a moral claim for its conclusion requires at least one relevant moral claim in the premises.

13.3. Universal Claims

Moral claims are usually held to be universal in nature. That is, they admit of few, if any, exceptions. This is because it is considered morally questionable to be inconsistent in applying moral standards. For instance, if Fred is forever chastising others for drinking alcoholic beverages by saying, "One should not drink alcoholic beverages," Fred is thought to be a terrible hypocrite if he is found to be a secret drinker. Such hypocrisy upsets all of us because we all tend to use moral rules as binding on all moral agents. This doesn't mean that there can never be exceptions to moral rules, but it does mean that such exceptions need to be justified by morally relevant criteria and reasons. (For instance, if the teetotaler Fred drinks alcohol only in the form of communion wine in church services, we would normally not see this exception to his attitude toward alcohol as being hypocritical. Here, the morally relevant criterion would be Christ's instructions to "Take and eat, take and drink.")

Thus, our next **rule of thumb** for assessing moral arguments is, Examine the argument or position for consistency. Are any exceptions made to universal moral conclusions? Are such exceptions justified by appeal to relevant moral criteria?

13.4. Conflicting Moral Claims

Because of our natural tendency to feel threatened by people who adopt moral positions different from our own, it is useful to recall that there can be—indeed, there usually are—good moral reasons for adopting more than one position on a moral issue. Thus, always treat your opponent in moral arguments with extra respect and charity. After all, moral problems would likely not be controversial if things were as clear and obvious as we often feel they are in ethical matters. It is because ethical rules can *conflict* in some situations that moral controversies are so difficult to handle. For instance, we all tend to feel that the taking of human life is to be avoided and also that we should promote the welfare of the living. But when faced with the issues of abortion and capital punishment, these moral rules come into conflict. Do we value the life of the fetus or the well-being of the mother? Do we value the life of the convicted murderer (who may, after all, be unjustly convicted) or the protection of the rest of society? Obviously, we value both values in each of these instances. Yet, when we are faced with a "devil's choice," we have to choose value against value. In such cases, it is often recognized that we should "choose the least evil," that is, decide which moral rule is more weighty in the current context, and why. When considering the "least evil" in a given situation, it is often useful to consider the overall effects of adopting each of the proposed courses of action. For instance, many argue that capital punishment is acceptable because of its deterrent effect upon potential criminals, while many others fear that legalized capital punishment will erode our feelings of reverence for human life.

Thus, when assessing arguments about a moral issue, it is useful to become aware of the good moral reasons on *both* sides of the issue at stake, and to recognize that we must choose between conflicting values, values that may very well be shared by persons on both sides of the argumentation. Choosing between such shared values is often extremely difficult: there is no simple way to decide. But it **promotes dialectic** to recognize the kind of choice involved in such cases; it is not a rejection of one or the other value but a decision that one of the values is more important in the given context. Thus, those in favor of capital punishment or abortion should not be characterized as evil persons not caring about the value of human life; in many cases, it is their concern with the quality of life of everyone in the society that influences their standpoint. (They may, of course, be wrong or unpopular without being evil or immoral.) This approach **promotes dialectic** by focusing the argumentation on the reasons for adopting one value in the face of a conflicting value. Conflicts of value should be used to promote humility in dialectic rather than self-righteous name-calling.

Thus, our final **rule of thumb** for assessing moral arguments is, Become aware of the moral reasons on both sides of a controversy, and recognize that the choice is often a matter of weighing two or more relevant moral beliefs and adopting the course of action that, in context, promotes the most good or the least evil.

CHAPTER 14

Assessing Arguments—Informal Fallacies

Informal fallacies are errors of reasoning that are context dependent, that is, they are semantically moored errors of reasoning. There are usually exceptions to informal fallacies—many will be pointed out subsequently. They are called "informal" because they rest in part on the content (in context) and not just on the form of the arguments.

Also, because our aim is to **promote dialectic,** the application of fallacies should be done in such a way as to lead to further discussion, not to end discussion. The object is not to say that an argument is bad or unacceptable but rather to show *how* or *why* an argument is not rationally persuasive (at least without further dialectical improvement). Therefore, when charging an argument with committing a fallacy, we must **argue** that the fallacy has been committed and we must show what conclusion or logical move is involved and why it is improper in the context of the current dialectic.

There is often overlap between fallacies since a particular move in a particular argument may in context be covered by several of the charges outlined in this section. In such cases, we should choose the charge that seems most likely to **promote dialectic.** Thus, the use of fallacies as aids in rational critique develops both offensive and defensive techniques. We must be defensive and learn to analyze the logic of others' arguments; but we must also learn to take the offensive to show why and how an argument or position fails to be rationally persuasive. This offensive move actually aids the dialectic, because it often both closes off unfruitful lines of development and opens up more promising ones. Above all, we should scrupulously avoid irrelevant or abusive use of rhetoric that tends to arouse emotions that make the dialectic degenerate into debate. Keeping this in mind, let us examine a number of informal fallacies.

Dos and Don'ts in Handling Fallacies

Because our goal is to use our knowledge of fallacies to promote dialectic, some tips can be helpful in knowing how this is to be done. Above all, remember that if you are arguing face-to-face with someone, a good **rule of thumb** is, never use the word *fallacy.* Remember the importance of making points in a "face-saving" manner through the use of **indirect rhetoric.** Rather than "You've committed the straw man fallacy!" (which will immediately put your interlocutor on the defensive), try something more like, "I'm not sure that I've understood you correctly. You have represented my position as [fill in the blank with their misrepresentation of your position], but that's not really what I meant—or believe . . . ." Then restate your position clearly and in different terms.

Also, remember that presence of fallacy doesn't "destroy" a position. Often, a "quick fix" can restore the argument's assertion to rational persuasion. For example, the charge of PROBLEMATIC PREMISE can often be replied to simply by offering available evidence.

Informal fallacies are called "informal" because they represent modes of reasoning that are not always fallacious or bad reasoning. **Every charge of fallacy must be defended by an argument.** Each such argument must have **two parts**. First, you must establish that the "argumentative move" relevant to a particular fallacy is present (for instance, if the charge is straw man, you must demonstrate that the person has restated an argument or position; if the charge is improper appeal to pity, you must demonstrate that there is an appeal to pity in the argument; and so forth). Second, you must **argue** that that particular use of the appropriate "argumentative move" is inappropriate (in this argument, in its context).

Argument to demonstrate that a fallacy is present:

1. Demonstrate that the "**argumentative move**" is present in the argument.
2. Argue **why** this move is **inappropriate** in this argument, in its context.

To summarize this discussion, consider the following table.

Dos	Don'ts
1. Use indirect rhetoric in face-to-face arguments.	1. Never use the word *fallacy* in a face-to-face argument.
2. Limit the "scope" of your charges: the presence of a fallacy in an argument does not by itself "destroy" the position in the conclusion.	2. Act as if a fallacy defeats a person's whole position.
3. Defend all charges of fallacy by argument.	3. Defend a charge of fallacy with a pseudo argument.
4. Include **both** steps in your argument: establish the presence of the "argumentative move," and argue *why* this move is inappropriate here.	4. Make a charge of fallacy without argument. (This would be committing the fallacy of *begging the question* by you!)
5. Be explicit.	5. Expect your audience to read your mind.
6. Avoid overreliance upon RQs, RIs, RCs, and UPs.	6. Expect your audience to produce your argument for you.
7. Use knowledge of fallacies to PROMOTE DIALECTIC.	7. Use knowledge of fallacies to bash your opposition.

Now we are ready to look at some individual fallacies.

14.1. Irrelevant Premise

Sometimes one offers as evidence for conclusion some premise, but that premise simply has nothing to do with the conclusion. In such cases, you may charge that the premise is an **irrelevant premise** that doesn't contribute to the acceptability of the conclusion. Of course, if your interlocutor shows a connection—in context—between that premise and conclusion that is relevant to the argument, then you must drop the charge of irrelevant reason. Note here the way in which a knowledge of fallacies may be useful in promoting dialectic.

14.2. Problematic Premise

Recalling the discussion early in section 2.1 about when premises should and should not be defended, you may charge **problematic premise** whenever you feel that (in context) a premise may not be true, that is, when you find a reason to believe a given claim may not be acceptable. This fallacy may be charged even if you cannot prove the falsity of the claim: "problematic" means "debated" or "a matter of controversy," not "false." To charge an argument with this fallacy, you must demonstrate that in context there is some reason to doubt the claim made in the premise.

This is sometimes a relatively weak charge in the ongoing dialectic. It really asks for more evidence. Often, the charge of problematic premise is replied to with sufficient evidence to support the premise. It may also be a strong charge; the further research required to reply to a charge of problematic premise may turn up evidence disproving the premise—or even the conclusion of the argument. This informal fallacy, when used properly, is invaluable to dialectic since it points out the weak links in our grasp of important matters.

When charging that a premise is problematic, it is not enough to say that "no evidence is provided" for the premise. Many premises do not need to be supported by evidence. To explain why a premise is problematic, one must show *why* evidence is required for a particular premise. This will require reference to the **context** of the argument. Nor is it enough merely to say that the premise is "debatable," since this is often stated *instead* of providing reasons for *why* it is debated. In other words, you must demonstrate why there is reason to doubt the premise. If it is well known that the issue is currently under debate, it is sufficient to support the charge of problematic premise by pointing out that the issue *is debated* (of course, you must judge your target audience to be aware of this debate).

It is sometimes hard to be sure when a premise requires defense. The following two rules should help you to make this decision.

> **Rule 1:** In general, each premise of an argument should be defended unless exempted by the context of the argument. A partial listing of situations justifying exemptions includes
>
> 1. If the premise is self-evidently true
> 2. If the premise asserts something that is a matter of common knowledge to the audience to which the argument is addressed
> 3. If the arguer has some special justification, status, or qualification for making that particular conclusion (e.g., if he or she is a recognized authority on the matter in question)

4. If the premise has already been defended elsewhere and that defense is referred to
5. If the arguer recognizes the need for defense of the premise and indicates a willingness to provide the defense later
6. If the premise is offered "for the purposes of argument," in order to show what follows (or might follow) from it

Rule 2: The more crucial and more controversial a premise is, the more serious is the failure to defend it.

14.3. Dubious Assumption

This is an unstated premise (UP) that is problematic, often a warrant.

14.4. Hasty Conclusion

This fallacy is charged whenever the evidence presented in the premises is insufficient to justify acceptance of the conclusion. Any invalid deductive argument commits this fallacy. Inductive arguments are often cited as being guilty of **hasty generalization**—a form of argument that generalizes from insufficient evidence. Both of these fallacies essentially ask for more evidence; thus, their use may **promote dialectic** in much the same way as do charges of "problematic premise."

14.5. Ad Hominem

This fallacy occurs when we attack our opponent(s) instead of the issues or arguments. **Ad hominem** attacks are very injurious to dialectic, for most of us respond to them emotionally. (We often speak of our thinking as "clouded by anger.")

14.6. Guilt by Association

Closely related to **ad hominem**, this fallacy consists in attacking an arguer or a cause by falsely linking it with someone or something that our audience responds to with automatic dislike. Thus, in different contexts, linking one with Communism, Conservatism, Stalin, or Nixon constitutes a fallacy of guilt by association.

14.7. Questionable Classification

This fallacy occurs when an argument classifies something (person, event, etc.) in a way that is unacceptable and then uses that classification as support for a conclusion.

14.8. Ad Populum

In this fallacy, the argument appeals not to reason or evidence but to emotion linking the conclusion rhetorically with some attribute of which the argument's audience will likely approve. Appeals such as "Loyal Americans know . . ." and "Successful executives have found . . ." sway people because they wish to be thought of as loyal and successful.

14.9. Fallacy of Flattery

This fallacy might be called the "democratic fallacy," after Plato's critique of democracy in his *Republic*. This fallacy occurs often in the political arena. It occurs when a speaker or writer flatters his or her audience instead of addressing the issues at hand.

14.10. Provincialism

Closely related to **ad populum,** this fallacy occurs when an argument employs as a premise some unreasonable belief that has been concluded either without evidence or with a selective look at the evidence, and that we believe that the most likely reason for this bias is the arguer's identification with some sociocultural group to which the arguer belongs (country, race, sex, culture, religion, etc.).

14.11. Blind Loyalty

This fallacy occurs when something or someone an arguer identifies with is attacked and the arguer either refuses the force of the evidence or denies the possibility of such evidence, and the most likely reason for this is the arguer's loyalty to the subject attacked.

14.12. Straw Man

This common fallacy occurs when one attributes to one's opponent a view different from that opponent's view and then attacks one's own parody instead of one's opponent's view. Thus, opponents of welfare often describe those in favor of welfare as supporting "a free ride for everyone who doesn't want to work!" (Surely this is an overstatement.)

14.13. Improper Appeal to Authority

Quite often, an argument appeals to a person or group who also accepts the conclusion (or a premise) in order to effect the audience's acceptance. This is often acceptable; after all, experts in a field will know more about their subject matter than others. But many appeals to authority are unacceptable. A few guidelines will help to spot these cases:

1. The authority appealed to must be a recognized expert in the appropriate field for the argument.
2. There must be an established domain of knowledge relevant to the conclusion with recognized criteria of truth or acceptability.
3. If experts in the appropriate field disagree, then the disagreement must be noted and the conclusion weakened accordingly.
4. The authority must not be in a position of bias or conflict of interest.
5. The authority must be identified.

When citing this fallacy, make sure that your argument attacks not the conclusion backed by the authority but the propriety of the appeal to authority itself.

14.14. Two Wrongs, Common Practice, Past Practice

These three fallacies are closely related. If a person or action comes under attack and someone supports that person or action by saying that someone else (or a group) also does the act or has the trait attacked and the fact that someone else does it is irrelevant to the defense of the person or action under attack, then the fallacy of **two wrongs** has been committed. We often hear people say, "Two wrongs don't make a right." Likewise, if common or past practice is appealed to as a defense and if this is irrelevant to the defense, the fallacy of **common** or **past practice** has been committed.

14.15. Questionable Cause

Many arguments rely upon causal conclusions that purport to show a causal link between things. The fallacy of **questionable cause** occurs when (1) an argument makes a causal claim that is unacceptable without further evidence; or (2) an argument recommends action or policy on the basis of a causal claim, and either (a) the causal claim is unacceptable or (b) the causal claim does not adequately support that action or policy.

Causal claims may go wrong in many different ways, but a few hints are helpful. First, look for the role of **induction** in causal claims. Many general causal claims are inductive. For example, because **R** followed **Q** many times in the past, they seem to be causally related; thus, we predict that if we bring about **Q, R** will follow. Induction requires strong evidence if the probability of the conclusion is to be strong or if the conclusion is controversial. Therefore, the **inductive leap** beyond the evidence given in arguments should be scrutinized carefully. Have many instances of R following Q been observed, or only one? Have other possible causes of R been ruled out? (This is the role of "control" in controlled experiments.)

One kind of causal fallacy is called **post hoc ergo propter hoc** ("after the fact therefore caused by the fact"). Because not every event that follows a given event **X** is necessarily caused by **X**, it is insufficient to conclude the presence of a causal link between two events merely because one follows the other. We all get up in the morning before we go to work, but our rising hardly **causes** our employment.

Causal claims often fail to be rationally persuasive because they cite one of many causes of something to be the only or the most important cause of it. For instance, a rise in interest rates often helps with other factors to bring about a rise in unemployment. Economists agree about this. But the experts disagree about how effective it is to try to manipulate interest rates in order to effect a change in the rate of unemployment. So, if an economist cites a recent rise in interest rates as the cause of a rise in unemployment, other economists could charge the argument with **questionable cause.**

It should be noted that "questionable" here does not mean "false." You need not prove that **Q** is *not* the cause of **R** to raise this challenge. What you must argue is that there is *reason to question* the conclusion that **Q** causes **R,** and here the **burden of proof** is upon the person making the challenge.

14.16. Wedge or Slippery Slope

This fallacy is a common form of **questionable cause**, relating two or more causal claims in an argument. It is committed when (1) it is argued that **A** leads to **B, B** leads to **C,** and so on to, say,

D; if (2) **D** is stated or assumed (this is a **UP** in most wedge arguments) to be undesirable; and (3) any causal link in the argument is a questionable cause.

14.17. Red Herring

This fallacy occurs when the argument "sidetracks" the dialectic, changing the subject to one that is unhelpful to the current dialectic. For example, watch politicians in press conferences; quite often, when they seem to change the subject or to talk forever without saying anything, it is because the issue just brought up is a touchy one they would prefer not to discuss.

14.18. Faulty Analogy

This fallacy occurs when an argument rests upon an analogy and there is reason to call the analogy itself into question.

14.19. Ambiguity

This fallacy occurs when a term or idea that is used in establishing the conclusion of an argument relies upon two different senses in the argument: one sense is used in the premise(s), but another sense is required to accept the conclusion. Consider the following example.

> P1: Americans value freedom.
> P2: Atomic bombs free electrons.
> ———————————————
> C: Therefore, Americans should drop atomic bombs.

Obviously, the political freedom that is valued in P1 only contributes to the desirability of the "should" in the conclusion if atomic bombs are linked to such political freedom. Instead, P2 relies upon a different sense of freedom—the freedom from physical restraint. Thus, this argument commits the fallacy of **ambiguity**.

14.20. Vagueness

This fallacy occurs when an argument contains a claim (or part of a claim) that is so vaguely worded that it is impossible to judge its acceptability as a premise or its significance as a conclusion. One should note here that one may think that a claim is vague due to one's own lack of knowledge; sometimes, what one thinks is vague is revealed to be clear when further information is revealed.

14.21. Begging the Question

This fallacy occurs when an argument contains a conclusion in its premises that cannot be accepted unless at the same time one would reasonably accept the conclusion. In obvious cases (in which the wording is obvious), it is often referred to as *arguing in a circle*, or *circular reasoning*.

14.22. Inconsistency

This fallacy occurs when the acceptance of an argument's premises and conclusion leads logically to the acceptance of two contradictory conclusions.

14.23. Improper Appeal to Pity

Sometimes an arguer appeals to the emotion of pity rather than to the issues. For instance, a man on trial for murder may try to make the jury feel sorry for his children who will be left without a father if he is convicted. Because the appeal to pity here is really a **red herring**, moving away from the issues of the trial, this would be an improper appeal to pity. Of course, not all appeals to pity are improper. When a charity or relief organization puts on a fund drive (in which they try to convince others to contribute to those in need), they often describe the pitiable plight of people to receive the benefits of personal contributions. This is a proper appeal to pity since pity here is a relevant issue.

14.24. Improper Appeal to Force or *Ad Baculus*

Because arguments are intended to persuade by *reason*, any appeal to force, whether overt ("Your money or your life!") or covert ("Senator, my firm represents a hefty voting block in your district"), is usually considered improper, given the proper circumstances.

CHAPTER 15

Summary of Argument Analysis

1. Find the conclusion of the argument.
2. Find the argument's premises.
3. Put the argument into logical structure.
4. Fill in any UPs or UCs required by the argument.
5. Ascertain the argument's validity or strength.
6. Judge the relevance of the premises.
7. Judge the acceptability of the premises.
8. Locate and argue for the presence of any informal fallacies.

Chapter 16

How to Produce a Good Argument

By looking at how arguments can "go wrong," logicians have learned a great deal about how to produce good arguments. The following good rules of thumb should be helpful.

1. Be sure that all your conclusions are true or at least acceptable.
2. Be sure that the evidence presented in your premises is relevant, acceptable, and sufficient to justify your conclusion (or its probable truth if the argument is inductive).
3. Double-check the sufficiency of your evidence; the most common mistake in arguing is overstating the conclusion. Strong conclusions may be justified only by strong evidence.
4. Introduce and reply to objections that have been or may be raised against your position.

This last point merits some discussion. It often happens that when you present an argument you expect a particular line of objection or counterargument. Some lines of objection are expected because they are often raised, and others because they are rather obvious objections to one's own argument (assuming your opponent's point of view). It can save a lot of time to raise such objections yourself and reply to them, thus taking the dialectic one stage farther. For instance, consider the following rather standard argument against capital punishment.

> Capital punishment should not be allowed. The government should not sanction the taking of human life in times of peace. We should use the government's power to reinforce our belief in the sanctity of human life. Mistakes are made by the courts, and capital punishment is irreversible. Innocent men and women will die from the practice of capital punishment.

Put into logical structure, this argument looks like this:

P1A: We should use the government's power to reinforce our belief in the sanctity of human life.
P1B: (RI) The American people believe in the sanctity of human life.
P1: The government should not sanction the taking of human life.
P2A: Mistakes are made by the courts.
P2B: Capital punishment is irreversible.

P2: Innocent men and women will die from the practice of capital punishment.
UP3: It is unjust to put innocent persons to death.
UP4: We should not do that which is unjust

C: Therefore, capital punishment should not be allowed.

Anyone presenting such an argument cannot help but be aware of the lines of argument most often raised by the "other side" in the debate over capital punishment, such as the "deterrent argument" and the "victim's rights" argument. Since the victim's rights argument requires the support of the deterrent argument (because having harsh laws won't serve the interests of potential victims unless such laws have a deterrent effect upon potential criminals), it is useful to raise the following and reply to the deterrent argument as a part of one's own argument against capital punishment.

> Many argue that capital punishment serves as a deterrent thus preventing potential crimes from occurring. But this is questionable. Studies in areas switching from the legal use of capital punishment to the abolition of capital punishment indicate no rise in crime when capital punishment was abolished.

Let's add this to our standardization:

P5A: Studies have been made in areas that switched from the legal use of capital punishment to the abolition of capital punishment.
P5B: These (P5A) studies show no rise in crime after capital punishment was abolished.
UP5C: If capital punishment were a deterrent, one would expect crime rates to rise when capital punishment was abolished.
P5 (RI): Capital punishment is not a deterrent to crime.

It would of course be more convincing actually to cite specific studies, which are vaguely referred to in P5A. Such evidence would be added as P5A1, P5A2, and so on. But note especially how the inclusion of P5A . . . P5 is a strategy that **promotes dialectic** by going one step farther, focusing attention on a serious disagreement (the debate over deterrence) and offering one's evidence on the issue.

CHAPTER 17

The Argumentative Essay

Although the main object of the course is to teach you to reason more effectively, we must not stop at this. A further goal is to help you to communicate the results of your reasoning more effectively. The overall structure and style of the argumentative essay will be dictated by our logical goal.

17.1. Structure

An essay that assesses or presents an argument must do more than just plunge into the argument. Like any essay, it should have an introduction, body, and summary (see outline in section 17.3).

17.1.1. Introduction

Your goal in the introduction is to acquaint your reader with a particular controversy in an argumentative context. A summary of the argument's **main** points, strengths, and weaknesses should be included in the introduction. The reader must also become acquainted with your "point," that is, what you are trying to get across in your own argument, your conclusion.

Remember that these points are merely introductory, introducing your reader to the subject of the paper and what points you plan to make about it; they should be expressed as briefly and as clearly as possible. Before you can make this kind of concise summary, you should determine the logical structure of the controversy and its arguments (in terms of the logical structure). Once this is clear, it becomes easy to summarize the main points. Work out the entire structure of the arguments to be presented in the essay (that is, construct their logical structures) **before** you start writing the essay! Also pay careful attention to the introductory and concluding sections of your essays, since first and last impressions color the way someone reads, understands, and remembers your points. If the controversy, the argument, and your point of view are set out clearly, it will make each step of the body of your paper more comprehensible. Clearly stating the importance of your point of view—what you see your argument as contributing to the ongoing dialectic—will give your reader a solid foundation for understanding the rest of your essay.

17.1.2. Body

As you write the main body of your essay, take a dialectical approach to your assessment. In other words, your job is not to attack an argument destructively but to criticize the argument in an open-minded search for truth based upon the issues and evidence in the context of the controversy. Your goal should be the improvement of your reader's understanding. (Remember that in a democracy, you owe it to your fellow citizen to argue dialectically whenever argument is appropriate.)

You will, of course, ascertain the validity or strength of the argument, judge the relevance and acceptability of the premises, and locate and argue for the presence of any informal fallacies.

When you are locating fallacies, keep in mind that the charge of fallacy does not usually refute a line of reasoning but expresses the need for more evidence. Also recall that informal fallacies are called "informal" because they are not always fallacious; there are appropriate circumstances in which to appeal to pity, force, popularity, and so on. Be fair. Argue with care for your fellow man.

Argumentative essays require you to present your own position. You will have noted vague impressions or underdeveloped arguments in your analysis of the controversy, and these impressions will help you to focus your argument. You should also test your argument against a variety of interpretive backgrounds or counter examples. The point is that you must fully explore what the issues are by testing your argument against opposing arguments—by testing your own beliefs and assumptions. In this way, you can determine what your unstated premises are and state them; this is one of the most difficult aspects of critical thinking. The best way to do this is to write down your thoughts. Start with just "key word" notes and work through *at least two drafts*, each time rethinking the arguments. (It is often necessary to produce new logical structures for successive drafts as you change your view of the topic.)

Do not be surprised if after this thorough testing your conclusion is not what you expected or desired. The good argument is the one that **promotes dialectic**, not the one with strong conclusions that are not rationally defensible. You will have made a contribution to the dialectic of the controversy if you have produced good reasons and evidence to support a smaller conclusion. This approach exhibits care and respect for the good parts of opposing views.

17.1.3. Summary and Conclusion

Now that you have analyzed the argument(s) and presented your own point of view, summarize the main points you wish to make. The conclusion of your own argument should be restated clearly and in context, along with the most important premises of your argument. Beware most especially against committing the following fallacies.

1. The "zinger punch line," which overstates what you have in fact proven, causing a hasty conclusion
2. The "zinger analogy," which is a faulty analogy
3. The "zinger one last swat at your opponent," which commits the straw man or the *ad hominem* fallacy

17.2. Style

Since the point of an argumentative essay is to convince the reader of something and since logical thinking is often rather complex, you must strive at all times to keep your expression simple, clear, and to the point. Naturally, you want to avoid vague "buzzwords," unexplained jargon, and clumsy sentence structure. But this sophisticated style rarely comes in the first draft of an essay. One of the most important elements in writing is learning the need for *drafting*.

A first-draft essay can be easy to identify. Its focus is usually egocentric, that is, it doesn't take the *reader* into consideration. Because of this, first-draft essays have been called "writer-based."[1] It is hard to think of your own text as a reader, but this is the key to effective writing: how will the reader interpret this? We need a first draft to get our ideas and arguments on paper. But then, with the second (or later) draft, we need to focus upon *communicating* our ideas to others. In writing for others, we have to be in control of language, of context, and of the realities of the communicative situation.

This does not mean that the first, or writer-based, draft should be scrapped. On the contrary, a writer-based draft is a rich groundwork of data for your argument. It will provide the basic premises and the clues to your unstated premises. Your task in the argumentative essay is to transform that groundwork into a reader-based draft. As you study your first draft, you may also begin to see subtle strategies in your argument that will clarify it to your reader. For instance, you may have originally seen your argument's logical structure as a chain of premises supporting a conclusion, but you begin to see from your writer-based draft that you actually have various clusters of smaller arguments supporting the conclusion. The writer-based draft is the foundation for the finished draft.

The logical structure of your argument should be evident throughout your finished draft. The logical structure will relate the various arguments and their parts to a central theme: the point of the essay. By focusing on this, you will be sure to present not only the various facts, values, and ideas of your discussion but how they are related. Good luck!

17.3. Outline of the Argumentative Essay

I. Introduction
   A. Introduce the topic of the controversy: What is at stake in the issue? What "sides" are argued either often or influentially?
   B. Introduce the argument(s) you are assessing: What are its main points? How does this argument fit into the controversy? (What does this argument lead to in the controversy?)
   C. Introduce your view. What "side" do you take or what compromise do you make in the controversy? What point do you want to make?

II. Body
   A. Assessment of argument
      1. **General comments** on the argument: Keep the argument in its context. Is it a good argument or a bad one or partly good and partly bad? A **GOOD argument** is one that contributes to a dialectical examination of a particular issue. Is it deductive or inductive? Why?
      2. **Specific comments** on the argument: What particular features of the argument either contribute to or detract from the dialectical examination of the subject? Is it valid? Are the premises relevant? Are the premises acceptable? Does the argument rely upon

---

[1]The idea of reader- and writer-based drafts is taken from Linda Flowers, "Writer-Based Prose: A Cognitive Basis for Problems in Writing," *College English* 41(1979): 19–37.

unstated assumptions? Does it raise any important points about the issue in question? Does it contain any fallacies?

B. Presentation of your position
    1. Summarize your conclusion and supporting premises. Have you noted possible refutations? Have you "reasoned the argument through" from more than one point of view?
    2. Explain your premises. Have you tried to discover and make explicit your own relevant assumptions and beliefs? Does your conclusion follow from your premises?

III. Summary
    A. Briefly restate the **main points** of your assessment of the main points of the argument (II A) within the context of the controversy.
    B. Briefly restate your position (II B) within the context of the controversy.

CHAPTER 18

Sample Arguments about Capital Punishment for Analysis

The following argumentative letters to the editor were turned in by students of earlier semesters. We will use them to practice analyzing arguments. *Please note* that most of the bibliographic references for these articles are incomplete—in many cases, they lack names, pages, and so forth. The sentences have been numbered for ease of reference.

(1) 1. The death penalty does not deter criminals because at the time the crime is done they do not expect to be arrested. 2. Also, since many offenders are mentally unbalanced, they do not consider the rational consequences of their irrational actions. (Pierre C. Haber, New York, NY: *Newsweek*, Oct. 31, 1983)*

(2) 1. Those who believe that capital punishment will bring an end to crime believe that war will bring peace. 2. Sick, deranged people like J.D. Autry cannot function in our society, so we should kill them. 3. Sounds like something someone called Hitler tried to do: get rid of all the undesirables. (Lawrence Schott, Gainesville, Fla.: *Newsweek*, Oct. 31, 1983)**

(3) 1. J.D. Autry's life of violence challenged my stomach, but not my convictions about capital punishment (SPECIAL REPORT, Oct. 17). 2. The ACLU resists the death penalty because it is simply another form of violence and criminologists argue that it doesn't deter killers. 3. Both ignore the retributive dimension of justice. 4. The fact is that the J.D. Autrys, like their cancer-cell counterparts, have gone wild, devouring society. 5. They have lost their right to life. (Larry G. Thompson, Rexburg, Idaho: *Newsweek*, Nov. 7, 1983)***

(4) 1. Capital punishment is not homicide just as a legally imposed fine is not theft. 2. Legal executions are not indicative of an uncivilized society where human life is not valued; rather, not to execute proven murderers degrades the value of the victim's life so brutally snuffed out. (Stacy R. Seldin, Flushing, NY: *Newsweek*, Nov. 7, 1983)[†]

(5) 1. This Session of the State Legislature will once again debate the death penalty. 2. I strongly urge that such a measure be enacted. 3. The greatest fear a human being has is loss of life. 4. If there is a death penalty, the criminal who takes a life faces losing his own. 5. Lack of the death penalty leads to indiscriminate mayhem and murder. 6. It demonstrates that our society is unable to deal effectively with the criminal. 7. The Death Penalty Bill Must Not Be Stalled Again. 8. It Must Be Enacted Now. (Unsigned, *NY Times*, Jan. 17, 1970 p. 22)

(6) 1. Steven Judy is a 24-year-old construction worker from Indianapolis. 2. In the spring of 1979 he stopped to help, or so she thought, a woman stranded with a flat tire. 3. Instead, he further disabled the car and offered her and her three young children a lift. 4. She was raped and strangled; the children were tossed in a creek where they drowned. 5. If Judy is electrocuted tomorrow, as scheduled, the State of Indiana runs no risk of executing the wrong man—which takes care of one argument against capital punishment. 6. Nor does Judy think his punishment is cruel and unusual: he has taken to citing Bible passages that indicate his fate is appropriate. 7. And to make sure that no one extends to him the humanity he denied his victims, he has refused to support an American Civil Liberties Union petition for clemency. 8. His contempt for life, it seems, is absolute. 9. But though [Steven Judy's] death may be, so far as one can gauge such imponderables, no loss to society, the manner of his dying is a blow to civilization. 10. To civilize is not only to nurture cultural and technological development, but to advance morality and justice out of a primitive state. 11. By that definition, the United States is a civilized country. 12. Mr. Judy is, for whatever reason, a barbarian. 13. A civilized country can afford to deal with people like him in other, wiser ways. 14. What it cannot afford is the return to the club implicit in responding to his brutality with the like. 15. To endorse execution, however understandable the impulse, is quite simply to come down to his level. (editorial, *NY Times*, Mar. 8, 1981, p. 18E)

CHAPTER 19

Further Example Arguments for Analysis

(1) (Background: letter to the editor, *Dallas Morning News,* 1983—Headline: Wheel of History Is Turning.) To the editors: 1. Under the U.S. Constitution, a U.S. representative is elected to represent the interest and philosophies of his or her district as expounded in the election process. 2. However, a majority of Democrats in the House are determined to ignore the Constitution. 3. They are telling members, "We do not care what your constituents want; you vote and do as we tell you, or else." 4. For 50 years they have taught, preached, and practiced envy, covetousness, and dependency. 5. History shows that all civilizations have followed this time table: (1) The people go from change to spiritual faith, (2) from spiritual faith to courage, (3) from courage to liberty, (4) from liberty to abundance, (5) from abundance to selfishness, (6) from selfishness to complacency, (7) from complacency to apathy, (8) from apathy to dependency, (9) from dependency back to bondage. 6. We are now in the 8th stage and progressing rapidly. (Brooks L. Harman, Odessa, Texas)*

(2) (Background: letter to the editor, *Ft. Worth Star-Telegram,* Oct. 14, 1982—Headline: Pornography.) 1. Regarding Danny M. Moon's Oct. 5 letter. 2. Mr. Moon is wrong when he states that pornography is protected by the First Amendment. 3. In Miller vs. California, the U. S. Supreme Court held that obscene materials are not protected by the First Amendment. 4. Some will argue that *Playboy* is not pornography. 5. A check of a dictionary quickly, and solidly, dispels that lie. 6. Pornography is "written or graphic material intended to excite lascivious feeling." 7. *Playboy's* only reason to exist is to make money, even if it destroys this nation. 8. Some say that pornography doesn't hurt anyone. 9. This lie is quickly dispelled. 10. It is a fact that many crimes have a root in pornography. 11. An example is the mass murderer in Houston several years back. 12. A search of his residence turned up stacks of pornographic material. 13. Ask the more than two dozen victims or their families if pornography doesn't hurt anyone. (Steven Stout, Fort Worth, Texas)**

(3) (Background: "Opinion" column *Ft. Worth Star-Telegram,* Sept. 23, 1982, when it was being discussed whether or not Ronald Reagan should run for a second term as president—Headline:

President Reagan's Age.) 1. It has been 18 years since Sen. Barry Goldwater ran for president and was buried in a Lyndon Johnson landslide. 2. Now he is as close to being a respected elder statesman as our nation has, as much so, probably, as any of the three living ex-presidents. 3. For that reason, as well as Goldwater's impeccably Republican and conservative credentials, it is noteworthy when he expresses doubts, out loud and for publication, about a second term for President Reagan. 4. Goldwater raises the question of Reagan's age, entirely separated from his performance in office, and raises it from the vantage point of one who is eight months older than the president and who has declared his own intention to leave the Senate when his term expires in 1986. 5. The president's age undoubtedly will be an issue if he does choose to seek a second term in 1984. 6. He is the oldest man ever to assume the office when he was inaugurated two years ago and would be three weeks away from his 74th birthday at the start of a second term in January 1985. 7. Whatever dangers to the nation exist in a chief executive of advanced age will be debated, and should be debated, as the 1984 elections approach. 8. The Democrats would be expected to bring it up. 9. Somehow, though, it becomes a more worthy and less purely political issue when raised by the grand old man of Reagan's own party, a man partly responsible for Reagan's emergence on the national political scene. 10. It is a subject for thought not only for the electorate and the politicians, but for the president himself.***

(4) (Background: letter to the editor, *Dallas Morning News* Oct. 4, 1982—Headline: Tell Me Why.) 1. To the editors: How can Carl Rowan, or any other man of perceptions, continue to insist that the Great Society programs have helped the lower classes—particularly blacks? 2. Just a block away from my place of business there is a ghetto composed of whites, blacks, and Mexicans. 3. These sad people never look for work (not once in two years has a person on foot come by and asked for work), but, rather, they sit around, smoke dope, drink, fight, and increase the illegitimate population. 4. Why, I wonder continually, do people like Carl Rowan and leaders in the Democratic Party want to increase this sad condition with more funds? 5. Will someone please tell me why? (James E. Ferguson, Denton, Texas)†

(5) (Background: letter to the editor, *Dallas Morning News* Sept. 18, 1982—Headline: Finger Pointing.) To the editors: 1. In your editorial "Soviet Pipeline: Hanging Tough," you stated: "Another favorable prospect—from Reagan's standpoint—is an agreement to permit on-site inspection of the construction so that any use of slave labor by the Soviets could be detected. 2. It's by no means certain the Soviets can build such a pipeline without slave labor." 3. We should be the last nation on the face of this earth to point the finger at any nation using slave labor. 4. This country was developed by indentured servants and African slaves. 5. The forests were cleared, the plantations made, the beautiful antebellum mansions erected, the levees built, all by slave labor. 6. The western portions of our mighty railroads were built with hungry Chinese coolies and the eastern portions with starving Irish immigrants. 7. No, we are in no position to point the finger at the Soviets, or any other nation, for using slave labor. (John W. Poteet, Sr., Colbert, Oklahoma)‡

CHAPTER 20

How to Learn to Think Critically

I. Master the basics.
   A. The basics: Argument, dialectic, premise, conclusion, validity, invalidity, truth, falsity, relevance, acceptability, sufficiency, and the basic form of the various fallacies
   B. Make sure you can APPLY these concepts to a variety of example arguments.

II. Learn to CRITIQUE arguments through PRACTICE.
   A. CRITIQUE: Finding the STRENGTHS and WEAKNESSES of arguments (learn to critique BOTH SIDES of an issue)
      1. Put the argument into its logical structure, including missing premises and or conclusions.
      2. Make general comments: Get a feel for the argument in its CONTEXT. In general, is it a good argument or a bad one or partly good and partly bad? A GOOD ARGUMENT is one that contributes to a dialectical examination of a particular issue
      3. Specific critique: What particular features of the argument either contribute to or detract from the dialectical examination of the subject in question? For example: Is it valid (or strong)? Are the premises relevant and acceptable? Does the argument rely upon any unjustified assumptions? Does it raise any important points about the issue in question? Does it contain any fallacies?
   B. PRACTICE: Offensive and defensive
      1. Offensive: Construct your own arguments on various topics.
         a. WRITE DOWN the arguments in logical form.
         b. Critique them.
      2. Defensive: Examine and critique arguments of others.

III. Learn to apply these methods to longer works.
   A. **Defensively**: Write book reports that sort out the logical structure of the books—do they state and achieve their aims? Are their analyses clearly and logically written? And so on.
   B. **Offensively**: Write papers that address a particular issue clearly and in logical order—with the "proper" use of rhetoric (for instance, state the conclusion you wish to achieve both at the start and the finish of your paper, utilize a dash of nonironic humor where appropriate, and so forth).

CHAPTER 21

"Error Messages" for Critical Thinking

The following is a list of abbreviations that I have used to correct student papers in practical logic. The list is useful as a guide to "what can go wrong" in standardizing and assessing arguments. Keep this list of possible errors in mind as you criticize arguments. It can be an invaluable aid in preparing for exams.

Abbreviation	Interpretation
better	The fallacy (or whatever) you've charged is acceptable, but it would be better to charge (or do). . . .
bg	This is BACKGROUND INFORMATION, not part of the argument.
BQ	You are BEGGING THE QUESTION here.
C	This is the CONCLUSION of the argument.
cc	This is a counterconclusion, not an argument.
c/f	You've used argument CONTENT to explain argument FORM.
con	You're being too picky here; the CONTEXT of the argument is such that you should not lay this charge.
f =	The proper fallacy here is. . . .
FP	Finish the premise: you've left out important information.
HAQ	You haven't answered the question.
inv	Invalid

MP	You've missed a stated premise.
MRI	Mention that this is a restatement of a rhetorical implication.
MRC	Mention that this is a restatement of a rhetorical command.
MRQ	Mention that this is a restatement of a rhetorical question.
nosplit	You should not have split this premise; by doing so, you have taken out a connection that is important for the argument.
NP	Not a proposition, a sentence fragment
P	This is a premise.
RC	This is a rhetorical command; state the implied proposition(s).
RI	This is a rhetorical implication; state the implied proposition(s).
RQ	This is a rhetorical question; state the implied proposition(s).
SA	You've missed or wrongly interpreted a subargument.
LS	You have not put the argument into logical structure.
SM	Straw man: your paraphrasing has changed the argument.
split	Split this premise into its separate propositions (and look for possible subargument).
U	(Placed in front of P or C): You did not note this as an UNSTATED premise or conclusion.
UC	You've missed an unstated conclusion.
unc	This is UNCLEAR.
UP	You've missed an unstated premise.
val	Valid
WC	Wrong conclusion
WD	Weak defense: A stronger argument is required to support your charge.
WW	Wrong warrant

CHAPTER 22

Glossary

The following definitions are geared toward argumentation. The definitions are therefore in many cases more narrow than the full definitions of the terms.

ad hominem: an informal fallacy in which one unacceptably attacks the character of one's opponent, rather than the issue(s) at hand

ad populum: an informal fallacy in which one unacceptably appeals to popularity or flatters one's audience

adversary debate: arguing solely to win the argument, at any cost and by any means

argument: an attempt to rationally persuade someone of something

argumentation: the living, ongoing process of presenting arguments to change minds rationally

argumentative move: an appeal to a particular form of reasoning (for example, an appeal to pity or authority, a definition, an attack upon a person, a use of analogy, a generalization, etc.)

audience: anyone witnessing an argument

audience, target: the person(s) that an arguer intends to convince

case, stated: a particular individual, thing, or event referred to explicitly in an argument, as a basis for inductive generalization or prediction

charity, principle of: a "rule of thumb" in interpreting arguments, according to which one looks for the *best* in an argument, to give it its fair hearing in the court of reason

conclusion: the point of an argument, what it sets out to prove

consistency: the lack of contradiction (whether implicit or explicit) in an argument

content: the subject matter of an argument

contradiction: the assertion and denial of the same thing

contradictories: two assertions that cannot both be true, and one of which *must* be true

contraries: two assertions that cannot both be true, but allowing other options

deduction: arriving at a conclusion on the basis of a conceptual connection between at least one general statement and another statement (general or particular)

dialectic: an approach to argumentation that seeks to establish the truth, or the best possible way to act, in an open-minded and cooperative way with one's argumentative "opponent"

epideictic: a form of rhetoric, celebrating an important event

ethos: the rhetorical attempt to establish one's credibility as an arguer

evidence: the relevant and logically related material presented in premises to establish a conclusion

example: a case or illustration used to illustrate a general point rather than used as a basis for an inductive generalization or prediction, or is used in deduction to represent general features of something

exigence: the reason(s) why one presents an argument

explanation: showing why something is the case

fallacy, formal: a mistake of reasoning in which, according to the form of the argument, the conclusion does not follow from the premises

fallacy, informal: a mistake of reasoning, closely resembling a proper form of reasoning, in which the statement or reasoning is unacceptable because of its content in its context

form: the relation between the premises and the conclusion(s) of an argument—either the conclusion follows from the premises, or it does not

ground: a premise that establishes basic evidential support for a conclusion

hermeneutic: involved with interpretation (from the ancient Greek word for "interpretation": *hermeneia*)

heuristic: an inventional technique, with more than one possible form or answer

holistic: based on a relation to or understanding of a large and complex whole and its parts

inconsistency: saying or doing (or a combination thereof) two contradictory things

induction: the use of example(s) to make a prediction or generalization; or, the use of analogy to establish a possible connection between something known and something partially unknown

inference: drawing a conclusion from premises

interpretation: figuring out the meaning of something, especially a text

irony: saying or doing just the opposite of what one means

logic: the normative science of argument

logical structure: a diagram displaying the logical structure of an argument

operator, logical: a symbol in formal logic that has a stipulated, well-defined meaning that does not change (just as the meanings of "=," "+," etc. do not change in arithmetic)

overstatement: saying one thing emphatically, when in fact implying its opposite

paradigm: a particularly good example or an outstanding case of something

paradox: an apparent contradiction

pathos: appeals to emotion in argumentation

plenitude, principle of: interpreting a text requires taking the *whole* of the text into consideration

polysemy: a noun meaning "many meanings"—most words in natural languages are polysemic; this is an important element in the work of interpreting texts

premise: information used to establish a conclusion

premise, unstated: information needed but unstated to connect stated (or sometimes, unstated but implied) premise(s) with a stated or implied conclusion

proposition: (in logic) a sentence that can be true or false

propositional variable: a symbol in symbolic logic used to represent propositions (in the same way that letters are used to represent numbers in algebra)

recursive: a process done again and again

reductio ad absurdum: a form of argument in which one derives an absurdity (often a contradiction) from the premises of one's opponent in an argument

rhetoric: the art of persuasion

rhetorical command: the use of a command to imply one or more propositions

rhetorical implication: something implied by something else that is stated explicitly

rhetorical question: the use of a question to imply one or more propositions

rhetorical structure: the order in which an arguer presents his or her sentences

syllogism: a deductive argument with two premises

Toulmin Model: a model for breaking arguments down into different sorts of premises and connecting ideas

understanding: grasping both the literal meaning of a text and its contextual implications

understatement: saying one thing very weakly, when in fact implying its opposite

warrant: a premise that connects one or more grounds to a conclusion

CHAPTER 23

Exercises

23.1. Numbering of Premises—Exercise

Strategy for using Exercise 23.1. Numbering of Premises in Chapter 23: You have learned in the section on the Toulmin Model that every argument, including every subargument, requires at least one ground, one warrant, and a conclusion. Thus, in this exercise, without even concerning yourself with the content of the premises and conclusions, you can see where a number of unstated premises are required.

(1) P1 ________________ C	(2) P1 P2A1 P2A P2 ________________ C	(3) P1A(G) P1B(G) P1 P2 ________________ C
(4) P16 P17A1 P17A P17 P18 ________________ C	(5) P12A1A P12A1 P12A P12B P12C	(6) P1 P2 P3A P3 ________________ C

(7)	**(8)**	**(9)**
P1 P2 P3A1 P3A P3 ———————	P1 P2A P2 P3A1 P3A P3 ——————— C	P1(G) P2(G) P3(G) ———————

Name: ______________________________ **Date:** ____________

23.2. Finding Missing Premises—Exercise

(1)
P1: George has a cold.

____

C: George should rest and drink fluids.

(2)
P1: George has a runny nose.

P2: George has a fever.

(3)

P1A: George has a fever.
P1B: George is wheezing.

P1: George has the flu and a slight case of pneumonia.

____

C: George should see the doctor.

(4)
(Spoken by a mother to her eight-year-old)

P1A: You are too excited.
P1B: You are talking too loud.
P1C: You are perspiring freely.

____

C: You should read for a while.

(5)

P1A: Glenn is broke.
P1B: Glenn wants a new car.

P1: Glenn should get a job.
P2: Pete wants to hire someone.

(6)
P1: Suzanne is broke.
P2: Money can be had by working or by robbery.
P3: Suzanne doesn't like to work.
P4: Suzanne likes going to jail less than working.

(7)
P1: Latesia wants an A in the class.
P2: Latesia has a 71 average in the class.
P3: Tomorrow's test is the final, worth 50 percent of the grade.

C: Latesia should study tonight.

(8)

P1A: Delores is on a diet.
P1B: Delores has an apple and a piece of pie.
P1C: Delores is hungry.

P1: Delores should eat the apple.
P2: If Delores eats the apple, she'll leave the core.
P3: Delores is a neat person.
P4: Delores can throw the apple core in the garbage or on the floor.

Name: ______________________________ Date: ______________

23.3. Example Short Arguments for Interpretation and Analysis

(1) Background: This is adapted from a real advertisement, responding to the controversy over food additives (chemicals that are added to foods in processing to preserve, increase shelf life, etc.).

1. What's wrong with adding chemicals to our foods? 2. There is nothing unnatural about chemical food additives. 3. Everything in nature is made of chemicals. 4. Our bodies, their cells, the food we eat—all are made of chemicals. 5. Doctors know that we need chemicals to grow and be healthy.

Name: ______________________________ **Date:** ____________

(2) Background: Spoken during a debate over smoking in public places

1. Those nonsmokers should leave smokers alone. 2. Anyone who spends his or her time on non-smokers' rights is ignoring more important matters. 3. To argue that nonsmokers have the right to clean air is to ignore the terrible pollution of our air by industry. 4. Smokers are just minding their own business, since they are doing something that doesn't hurt anyone else.

Name: ______________________________ **Date:** ____________

(**3**) Background: Fictitious letter to the editor during a senatorial campaign

1. Why would anyone want to vote for Senator Snodgrass? 2. His conduct has been bad for the Texas economy. 3. Why, I visited Washington and saw him sleeping during the debate on the Supercollider. 4. The man votes like he sleeps through every debate. 5. He has flip-flopped on almost every issue on the docket.

Name: ______________________________ **Date:** ____________

(4) Background: Spoken during a debate over tax revenues

1. If we raise taxes, it'll be a disaster for the economy. 2. People will have less to spend, small businesses will fail, people will be without jobs, and this will shrink the tax base, so raising taxes will actually lower revenues.

Name: ______________________________ **Date:** ____________

(5) Background: Spoken to a friend who is in the market for a new car

1. You should buy the Speedo Supreme. 2. It is a fine automobile. 3. It is dependable, with the tried-and-true hydraulic suspension and an award-winning automatic transmission. 4. It is inexpensive to operate. 5. Why, in independent road tests, it beat both the Ford and the Toyota for gas mileage. 6. It goes ten thousand miles without a change of oil and is aerodynamically designed. 7. Furthermore, it comes with a super sound system.

Name: ______________________________ **Date:** ____________

(6) Background: Spoken during a debate over whether or not to allow the sale of genetically altered fruit in grocery stores

1. If we allow genetically altered fruit to be grown outside the laboratory, its spores can mix with the spores of other plants, both wild and domesticated. 2. When plants cross-pollinate, it can produce new species with unforeseeable properties. 3. So we might be bringing about the very shortage of food that the genetically altered foods were made to prevent.

Name: ______________________________ **Date:** ____________

(7) Background: Spoken at a discussion of organic gardening

1. Food additives should be banned. 2. Dumping chemicals in our food has affected the health of the entire nation. 3. Why, everyone knows that the incidence of cancer has increased ever since food additives have been placed into our diet.

Name: ______________________________ **Date:** ____________

(8) Background: Spoken in the University Center cafeteria

1. College parking should be free and handy for students. 2. The students are the ones that need to get to class, so they should be allowed to park close to their classrooms. 3. After all, they are the ones that pay for all this. 4. The faculty, staff, and administration are working for the students, so they should be the ones to have to take buses from remote lots and pay for all the parking.

Solution to even-numbered examples for Exercise 23.1 Numbering of Premises in Chapter 23:

(2) There are two main premises, P1 and P2. We don't know if they are grounds or warrants; thus, there need not be a UP3 required, if P1 is a ground and P2 is a warrant (or vice versa). However in the subarguments (P2A1, P2A), in both cases, there is only one premise. Thus, you should know that you need to add a UPA2, and a UP2B—you should also suspect that these unstated premises will probably (not necessarily!) be warrants.
(4) This example is just like example 2, except that the premises are numbered differently. You must add a UP17A2 and a UP17B (again, most likely warrants).
(6) You need to add a UP3B, probably a warrant.
(8) You need to add a UP2B, a UP3A2, and a UP3B, probably warrants.

Solutions for Exercise 23.2. Finding Missing Premises in Chapter 23:

(1) UP2(W-Principle): If one has a cold, one *should* rest and drink fluids.
(2) UP3(W-sign): A runny nose and fever are *signs* of a cold/flu.
UC: George has a cold or flu.
(3) UP1C(W-Sign): Fever and wheezing are *signs* of flu or pneumonia.
UP2(W-Principle): If one has pneumonia one *should* see the doctor.
(4) UP1D(W-Sign): Excitation, loud talk, and free perspiring are *signs* of the need to settle down.
UP1(W-Principle): You should settle down.
UP2(G): Reading will help to settle you down.
(5) UP1C(W-Principle): If one is broke and wants a car, then one *should* get a job.
UP3(W-Principle): If one wants a job one should talk to one who has a job opening.
UC: Glenn *should* talk to Pete.
(6) UP5(W-Principle): One *should* do the lesser of evils.
UC: Suzanne should get a job.
(7) UP4(G): Letesia needs an 'A' on the final exam.
UP5(W-Principle): If Letesia needs an 'A' on the final, then she *should* study tonight.
(8) UP1D(G): Pie is more fattening than an apple.
UP1E(W-Principle): When dieting, one *should* eat less fattening food.
UP5(W-Sign): Throwing the apple core in the garbage is a sign of being neat.
UC: Delores will throw the apple core in the garbage.

CHAPTER 24

A Request

I have been working on this text for many years, and I have always valued suggestions from students about what I am doing correctly and incorrectly, both in the text and in the classroom. Therefore, in addition to my usual course evaluation, I am asking you to supply me with your further suggestions about this text. I would appreciate it if you would take a few minutes to write on this page what *works* for you in this text and what *doesn't work* for you. I have modified the text as the result of many former student comments. I value and appreciate your advice. Please fill in the appropriate comments and turn in this text evaluation along with the course evaluation. Like the course evaluation, these comments will be anonymous and will not be seen by me until after I have turned in your grades. Thank you for your time. (Page numbers would be very helpful, when appropriate.)

Words to add to Glossary:

What in this text was **helpful** for me:

What in this text was **unhelpful** for me: